Langenscheidts Grammatiktraining Englisch

von Gabi Galster und Sigrid Brugger

Langenscheidt
Berlin · München · Wien · Zürich · New York

Langenscheidts
Grammatiktraining Englisch

von Gabi Galster und Sigrid Brugger

Herausgegeben von der Langenscheidt-Redaktion
mit Mitwirkung von Liam Cleary

Ergänzende Hinweise, für die wir jederzeit dankbar sind,
bitten wir zu richten an:
Langenscheidt-Verlag, Postfach 40 11 20, 80711 München

1. 2. 3. 4. 5. 05 04 03 02 01

Druck: Druckhaus Langenscheidt, Berlin
Printed in Germany – ISBN 3-468-**34941**-6

Vorwort

Übung macht den Meister! – Unter diesem Motto bieten wir Ihnen unser ***Grammatiktraining Englisch*** an. Hier finden Sie **mehr als 150 Übungen** zu den wichtigsten Themen der englischen Grammatik, wie z. B. **der *ing*-Form oder den *Phrasal Verbs*.**
Dieses Buch eignet sich gleichermaßen für Anfänger und Fortgeschrittene. Sie können es zum Lernen oder zum Auffrischen benutzen und so Ihr Englisch perfektionieren.

Die Übungen wurden speziell auf Ihre Bedürfnisse zugeschnitten.
Der übersichtliche Aufbau und die zweifarbige Gestaltung ermöglichen eine schnelle Orientierung. Da die Beispielsätze auf der **Alltagssprache** und einem **einfachen Wortschatz** basieren, bleibt Ihnen mühsames Nachschlagen schwieriger Vokabeln erspart.
Die Übungen sind so angelegt, dass Sie sie **schriftlich im Buch** lösen und mithilfe des **Lösungsschlüssels** sofort kontrollieren können. Dadurch ist das Buch besonders geeignet für das **Selbststudium.**

Übrigens: Falls Sie einmal etwas nachschlagen möchten, empfehlen wir Ihnen ***Langenscheidts Praktische Grammatik Englisch*** und ***Kurzgrammatik Englisch.***

Und nun wünschen wir Ihnen viel Spaß beim Grammatiktraining!

Autorinnen und Verlag

Inhaltsverzeichnis

1 Die Gegenwart: einfache Form und *ing*-Form

1 Die 3. Person Singular der einfachen Gegenwartsform hat unterschiedliche Endungen. Ordnen Sie die folgenden Verben in die richtige Spalte ein!

rely ✔ carry rush fetch mix show buy lie relax marry say copy grow

Endung	-es	-ies	-s
	....	*relies,*	....
	....	....	....
	....	....	....

2 Die fünf klassischen Verwendungen der einfachen Gegenwart – vermerken Sie im Kästchen, welcher Regel der jeweilige Satz folgt.

a Allgemeine Tatsachen
b Persönliche Fakten
c Natürliche Gesetzmäßigkeiten
d Sprichwörter
e Regelmäßig wiederkehrende Handlungen

1 My lunch break is at twelve thirty. ☐
2 The restaurant opens at 9 am and closes at midnight. ☐
3 In the United States shops tend to be open 24 hours a day. ☐
4 Too many cooks spoil the broth. ☐
5 I grow flowers on my balcony. ☐
6 As a professional football player you earn a lot of money. ☐
7 My girlfriend buys expensive clothes. She thinks they last longer. ☐
8 When in Rome, do as the Romans do. ☐
9 In summer, days are longer than in winter. ☐

3 Und nun das Gleiche für die Verlaufsform. Vermerken Sie im Kästchen, welche Regel dem jeweiligen Satz zugrunde liegt.

a Noch nicht abgeschlossene Handlungen über einen gewissen Zeitraum
b Gerade ablaufende Handlungen
c Allgemeine Zustandsveränderungen
d Zukunft: Etwas ohnehin Vorgesehenes wird eintreten.
e Unerfreuliche Prognosen bzw. Fragen höflicher gestalten

1 Your pancakes are getting better and better. ☐
2 I'm drinking a glass of water. ☐
3 We're leaving for France tomorrow. ☐
4 I'm usually preparing lunch when the kids come home from school. ☐
5 For the time being I am sharing a flat with my brother. ☐
6 His health is gradually deteriorating. ☐
7 ● What are you doing? ▲ I am cleaning the kitchen. ☐
8 I am sorry, but I can't answer the phone right now. I'm taking a shower. ☐
9 I'm afraid I am not supporting you in this matter. ☐

4 Entscheiden Sie sich für das einfache Präsens oder die Präsens-Verlaufsform.

to play As a professional tennis player, my brother ...*plays*... tennis regularly. I'm afraid you can't talk to him right now, because he .... ① a match right now. I'm sure it'll be over in an hour or so. He .... ② against our grandfather, you see. In summer they .... ③ twice a week.

to rain Look, it .... ④. What a shame! We can't go for a walk now. You don't mind the weather, do you? You're used to it. In Scotland, where you come from, it always .... ⑤ at this time of the year.

to stay My husband is in London at the moment. He .... ⑥ at the Savoy Hotel. He normally .... ⑦ there when he's in London.

work/not ● My computer .... ⑧. I've had it for five years now. Never a problem. But yesterday it broke down. May I use your computer?

▲ I'm afraid my computer .... ⑨. In fact, it hasn't worked for years.

to write I .... ⑩ a new novel. I never .... ⑪ short stories. I'm not good at expressing myself in so few pages.

to bake Whenever I visit her, grandmother .... ⑫ a cake. I never .... ⑬ cakes. My neighbour .... ⑭ biscuits every Saturday. She always .... ⑮ some for me.

5 Erneut die Frage: Präsens oder Präsens–Verlaufsform? Beachten Sie, welche Signalwirkung von *always*, *usually*, *regularly* ausgeht. Achten Sie auch auf die richtige Stellung des Adjektivs!

1 You are such a messy person. You .... (to leave / always) your things around.

2 Our neighbour downstairs .... (to complain / always) about us. He doesn't like the music we're playing. And it's too loud, he says. Listen, he .... (to play / now) the saxophone. He .... (to play / usually) the sax at about 5 o'clock. That man has such a nerve!

3 He .... (to go away / always) for weekends leaving his wife and kids alone. The poor woman. Well, my husband .... (to go away / regularly) for weekends, too. But I don't mind. I enjoy having the weekends for myself.

4 We .... (to have / always) roast beef on Sundays. Why can't we have pork for a change. I am sick and tired of beef. My mother .... (to serve / always) chicken on Sundays. I think Sunday is a good day for chicken.

6 „Zu Gast bei einer exzentrischen Familie – ein Gespräch nach Mitternacht“ – Einfaches Präsens oder Verlaufsform?

● *the guest* ▲ *the host*

● Who *is making* (to make) that terrible noise?

▲ It .... (to be) ① our grandfather. He sometimes .... (to practise) ② the violin at night. He .... (to play /not) ③ well, does he?

● But it .... (to be) ④ after midnight. Surely, he .... (to make) ⑤ too much noise?

▲ Oh, that noise .... (to matter / not) ⑥. We .... (to be) ⑦ all used to it. Look, the moon .... (to shine) ⑧ brightly. Grandad .... (to be) ⑨ moonstruck, you see. Sometimes he .... (to go) ⑩ swimming in the moonlight, or he .... (to dig) ⑪ holes in the garden.

● Listen, it .... (to get) ⑫ noisier and noisier.

▲ That is just my father. He .... (to snore) ⑬. Dad always .... (to snore) ⑭. But I .... (to warn) ⑮ you. There .... (to be) ⑯ more to come. My brother .... (to talk) ⑰ in his sleep and my little sister .... (to be) ⑱ a real sleep-walker.

● I think your sister .... (to walk) ⑲ around now. I can hear her steps.

▲ No, no, these .... (to be) ⑳ our family ghosts. I haven't told you about them yet. They .... (to dance) ㉑ upstairs in the attic. We .... (to call) ㉒ them Fred and Ginger because they .... (to love) ㉓ dancing. They .... (to be) ㉔ extremely polite. Sometimes they even come down and talk to us.

● You .... (to joke) ㉕, aren't you? You .... (to tell / not) ㉖ the truth.

▲ I always .... (to tell) ㉗ the truth. Listen, someone .... (to knock) ㉘ at the door. I .... (to wonder) ㉙ who that can be.

2 Die Vergangenheit *(Past Tense)*: einfache Form und *ing*-Form

1 Ordnen Sie die Verben in die richtige Spalte ein!

walk ✔ play reply travel suffer plug ✔ pull prefer listen
marry watch try label hurry benefit

Endung -ed	(Verdoppelung)-ed	-y > -ied
walked, ...	*plugged,*	....
....	....	....
....	....	....
....	....	....

2 Savoir vivre! – Wählen Sie das passende Verb aus, bilden Sie die einfache Vergangenheit und vervollständigen Sie damit die Sätze.

disappear encounter live marry ✔ move pour prefer scrub
suffer unplug use

1 I *married* my wife in 1955. She .... in France when she was a teenager. That's where she .... the French style of savoir vivre.

2 At the beginning of our marriage I always .... dusting the furniture to doing the washing up.

3 I .... from a dreadful backache. But when we .... into our new house and bought a new hoover the pain ....

4 Yesterday I .... the floor for hours, and it still looks filthy.

5 By mistake I .... a bucket of water over the TV set. But I .... the TV immediately.

6 I .... to lead a boring life before I met her.

3 Bilden Sie aus den angegebenen Substantiven das jeweilige Verb und setzen Sie es in der einfachen Vergangenheit ein.

collection loss meeting miss panic tip try walk wedding ✔

1 My father always .... to work.

2 I .... my wife at a party. We *married* one year later.

3 My boss is a very quiet person, but yesterday he .... his patience.

4 My grandpa .... stamps. Now they are worth a fortune.

5 When the fire broke out, people ....

6 Yesterday evening everyone .... the waiter generously. He was very nice and deserved a good tip.

7 Normally, my brother always scores during a basketball game. But in the decisive match he .... too hard. He .... five times.

4 Ihr *Yellow Langenscheidt-Cocktail* war ein voller Erfolg auf der gestrigen Party. Erklären Sie, wie Sie ihn gemacht haben!

You need:

1 melon
1 grapefruit
2 lemons
water
sugar
mint leaves
lemon twists

Halve a melon and remove the seeds. Make melon balls with a scoop and chill them.
Peel a grapefruit with a sharp knife. Cut the fruit into segments. Sprinkle the grapefruit segments with sugar. Allow them to stand at room temperature for 30 minutes.
Grate enough rind from two lemons to give 2 tablespoons. Squeeze the juice of 2 lemons. Add the grapefruit and melon balls, then purée everything in a blender.
Add enough water to give half a litre of liquid. Stir well. Taste and add sugar if desired.
Serve the cocktail in frosted glasses. Sprinkle the glasses with lemon grind. Garnish the cocktail with green mint leaves and a slice of lemon.

How I made that gorgeous cocktail? Well, I halved a melon and removed the seeds. Then ...

5 „Ein typischer Tag im Leben einer Hausfrau“ – Einfache Form oder Verlaufsform? Verbinden Sie die beiden Sätze.

1	I cleared the breakfast table.	My husband left for work.
2	I did the ironing.	I watched TV.
3	I took the dog out for a walk.	I thought about a nice birthday present for my mother-in-law.
4	I remembered that I had to pick up clothes at the dry–cleaner's.	I put the dirty clothes into the washing machine.
5	I made the beds.	I listened to the radio.
6	I worked in the garden.	The postman rang the doorbell.
7	I cleaned the windows.	It started raining.
8	I hoovered the flat.	I realized it was time to think about dinner.
9	I looked through my cookery book.	I discovered a nice recipe for fish and chips.
10	I peeled the potatoes and cut them into sections.	My mother dropped in for a cup of tea.
11	I laid the table.	My husband came home from work.
12	I opened a bottle of wine.	He sat at the table and looked forward to his dinner.

1 *While I was clearing the breakfast table my husband left for work.*

2 ....

3 ....

4 ....

5 ....

6 ....

7 ....

8 ....

9 ....

10 ....

11 ....

12 ....

6 *An evening with Lord Sinclair.* Lesen Sie, was Lord Sinclair für gewöhnlich tut, wenn er einen Abend im Theater verbringt.

Once a week Lord Sinclair goes to the theatre. On these occasions he always wears his morning suit. It consists of a long black coat, striped trousers and a waistcoat. He loves wearing a white shirt and a grey tie with his morning suit. Two hours before the start of the play he gets dressed. His butler prepares his top hat and cleans his shoes. Lord Sinclair has a glass of port in the library, and then his chauffeur drives him to the theatre. He takes his seat in the family box and follows the first act. During the break between the first and second act he has a glass of champagne. After the second act he always calls his mother to tell her about the play. When the curtain falls he usually feels hungry. After the performance he has supper at his club. Afterwards he and his friend play a game of bridge. Then he returns to his flat and goes to bed.

7 Vervollständigen Sie nun das Telefonat, das er am Tag nach einer Vorstellung mit seiner Mutter führt.

● *Lord Sinclair's mother* ▲ *Lord Sinclair*

● Did you go to the theatre last night?

▲ Yes, of course I ...went... to the theatre.

● Why didn't you call me?

▲ I .... ① you because I .... (to fall asleep) ② during act two. The play .... (to be) ③ very boring.

● Did you wear your morning suit?

▲ Yes, I .... ④ my morning suit with the long black coat, the striped trousers and my waistcoat.

● Did you wear a white shirt and a grey tie?

▲ Yes, I .... ⑤ a white shirt and a grey tie.

● Did James prepare your top hat?

▲ Yes, he .... ⑥ my top hat, and as always he also .... ⑦ my shoes.

● Did you have a glass of port in the library before you .... (to leave) ⑧?

▲ Yes, I .... ⑨ my usual glass of port. Benton .... ⑩ me to the theatre.

● Did you take a seat in the familiy box?

▲ Yes, of course I .... ⑪ a seat in the family box.

● Did you have a glass of champagne after the first act?

▲ I'm afraid I can't remember how many glasses of champagne I .... ⑫. All I remember is that I suddenly .... (to feel) ⑬ very tired. After the second act, Humbert .... (to wake up / me) ⑭ up. I immediately .... ⑮ to the flat and .... ⑯ to bed.

● You must have a double then. I just .... (to talk) ⑰ to Lucinda, and she told me that her niece, whom I dislike very much, as you know, ... (to spend) ⑱ a wonderful evening at the Ritz yesterday with someone who .... (to look) ⑲ exactly like you.

8 Ergänzen Sie die Tabelle.

Infinitiv	3. Pers. Präs.	*ing*-Form	einfache Vergangenheit
			said
to choose			
	tries		
			did
		having	
		eating	
to hope			
			supplied
to begin			
	develops		
			agreed
to argue			

3 Die einfache Vergangenheit und das *Present Perfect*

1 Fragen über Fragen! Die Formen des *Past Participle,* die Sie in dieser Übung brauchen, sind alle identisch mit der einfachen Vergangenheit.

buy ✔ feed have ✓ hear ✓ make ✓ pay ✓ read ✓ spend ✓ travel

Money, money, money

1 What type of car have you bought?
2 How much money have you .... for the car?
3 Have you .... all your money on a new limousine?

Leisure time and food

4 How many Italian operas have you .... recently?
5 What American short stories have you ....?
6 When have you .... lunch today?
7 Have you .... coffee yet?
8 Has he .... the cats?
9 Have you often .... by boat?

2 Jetzt wird es etwas komplizierter, denn die einzufügenden Formen stimmen mit der einfachen Vergangenheit nicht überein.

1 How many times have you .... (to be) to the theatre this month?
2 What colour have you .... (to chose) for your new car?
3 How many banks have you .... (to rob)?
4 Where have you .... (to hide) the money?
5 Have you ever .... (to eat) snails?
6 How many bottles of champagne have you .... (to drink) this week?
7 Have you .... (to see) the latest Stephen Spielberg movie?

3 *A hypochondriac's checklist.* Ordnen Sie den jeweiligen Krankheitssymptomen die „richtige" Ursache zu!

1 My eyes are sore.
2 I've got a stiff neck.
3 My breath smells.
4 I'm feeling tired.
5 My back aches.
6 I've got indigestion.
7 I'm coughing.
8 I'm suffering from a hangover.
9 My feet hurt and I have several blisters.
10 I've got sunburn.
11 I've caught a cold.
12 I'm sweating.

do too many stretching exercises
smoke too many cigarettes
sunbathe all day
eat too many garlic and onion canapes
walk in the rain
watch television all night ✔
not get enough sleep
carry heavy shopping bags
spend too much time sitting at the computer
eat too many chocolates
walk around in high heels all day
drink too much

I am so miserable!

1 My eyes are sore *because I have been watching television all night.*
2 I've got a stiff neck ....
3 My breath smells ....
4 I'm feeling tired ....
5 My back aches ....
6 I've got indigestion ....
7 I'm coughing ....
8 I'm suffering from a hangover ....
9 My feet hurt and I have several blisters ....
10 I've got sunburn ....
11 I've caught a cold ....
12 I'm sweating ....

4 *For* und *since* – ergänzen Sie die Verben in der korrekten Form: *einfache Vergangenheit* oder *Present Perfect*?

to live	I …………… ① here for the past 15 years. I love this part of town and I enjoy living here. Hemingway also …………… ② here for two years – from 1944 to 1946.
to move, to be able to	Since we …………… ③ to London in 1960, I …………… ④ to improve my English.
to attend	I …………… ⑤ evening classes for 2 or 3 months now.
to smoke/not	My mother …………… ⑥ for several days.
to see	We …………… ⑦ him a fortnight ago, but nobody …………… ⑧ him since.
to go, to be	It is a long time since we …………… ⑨ dancing together, isn't it? In fact, I don't think we …………… ⑩ to a disco for more than ten years.
to be, to turn up/not	I …………… ⑪ waiting here for more than an hour. But my mother …………… ⑫ yet, so I'm still sitting here.

5 Einfache Vergangenheit oder *Present Perfect*? Achten Sie auf die unterstrichenen Signalwörter!

1 Some time ago my father had (to have) a stroke. He has recovered (to recover) now.

2 Last year my parents …………… (to stay) at home during their holidays. But this year they …………… (to make) a trip around the world.

3 I …………… (to lose) his address and …………… (to find/not) it yet.

4 I …………… (to see/not) my brother since last Christmas.

5 David, why …………… (to come/not) for breakfast this morning?

6 I …………… (to finish) just …………… my translation.

7 …………… (to be) you ever …………… to the USA? Yes, last week I …………… (to visit) New York.

6 *The job interview.* Vervollständigen Sie dieses Bewerbungsgespräch. Wählen Sie zwischen Präsens, *Present Perfect* und einfacher Vergangenheit.

● *Ms Callman, Head of the Personnel Department* ▲ *Maria*

● Tell me something about your work experience.

▲ I worked (to work) for John Baxter Ltd. for about 10 years.

● Your English is good. You .... (to live) ① here for a long time, haven't you?

▲ Yes, I .... (to live) ② here for the past 16 years.

● Your surname is Sanchez. That sounds Spanish.

▲ Yes. My family .... (to be) ③ Spanish. I .... (to be) ④ born in Madrid.

● What does your father do?

▲ He .... (to be) ⑤ a teacher, but he .... (to work/not) ⑥ at the moment.

● How long .... (to be) ⑦ learning French?

▲ I .... (to be) ⑧ taking French lessons for 2 years now.

● What about German?

▲ I .... (to begin) ⑨ learning German 6 months ago.

● How many times .... (to change) ⑩ your job?

▲ I .... (to have) ⑪ three jobs since I .... (to leave) ⑫ school.

● Well, thank you very much. I'll call you tomorrow.

7 Ein Streitgespräch. Verwenden Sie die *Present Perfect*-Verlaufsform.

● *the husband* ▲ *the wife*

● Do you realize that we have been quarrelling (to quarrel) ever since we got married.

▲ Well, I .... (to ask) ① you to mend the roof for at least 5 years.

● Which means that we .... (to argue) ② about this roof for more than 5 years.

▲ That's because you .... (to listen/not) ③ to anything I said during our marriage.

● Ever since we met you .... (to try) ④ to boss me around.

▲ And you .... (to neglect) ⑤ me ever since you started your job.

4 Das *Past Perfect*

1 Einfache Vergangenheit oder *Past Perfect*? Ergänzen Sie die passende Form.

All the things that can go wrong if you are a scatterbrained person!

1 I .... (try) to open the door to the flat for half an hour when I suddenly noticed that it was my neighbour's door, not mine. No wonder the key didn't fit.

2 I .... (search) for my glasses all morning when I realized that I had them on. I .... (wear) them all the time without noticing.

3 It .... (rain) all day long when I remembered that I .... (forget) to take the washing inside. So I couldn't wear my pink dress for the party that evening because it was still soaking wet. It served me right.

4 I had a date with my new boyfriend. We .... (arrange) to meet in a pub. I .... (wait) there for half an hour wondering why he .... (not turn up) when it occurred to me that we wanted to meet at a pub called The Wellington and not at The Nelson.

5 I .... (shop) around for quite some time when it suddenly dawned on me that I .... (forget) to turn off the lights of the car. I went back to the car. The car battery was too weak. I couldn't get the car started. My brother had to pick me up.

6 I .... (enjoy) the first half hour of a beautiful film at the cinema with popcorn and Coke when I remembered that I might .... (forget) to turn off the cooker in the kitchen. I left the cinema in a hurry and raced home, straight into the kitchen. Everything was o.k. I .... (forget) to turn off the cooker after all. How stupid of me!

7 I .... (walk) up and down the road for quarter of an hour wondering where on earth I .... (park) the car when I remembered my husband telling me that he needed it that day. What a waste of time!

2 „Der Partyschreck" – Chronik eines katastrophalen Abends … Erzählen Sie den Ablauf!

1	He ate most of the party sandwiches.	All the other guests arrived.	BY THE TIME
2	He ate too much.	He was sick.	BECAUSE
3	He forgot to dance with his girlfriend.	She was very angry and decided to ignore him all evening.	BECAUSE
4	He spilt some red wine.	A horrible stain appeared on the white table cloth.	WHEN
5	He drank too much at the party.	He couldn't go home by car and had to walk home.	BECAUSE
6	He annoyed so many people at the party.	Nobody wanted to drive him home.	BECAUSE
7	He forgot to put on his coat and it was raining.	He got soaking wet.	BECAUSE
8	He remembered that he carried a raincoat in his rucksack.	He caught a cold.	BY THE TIME
9	He walked ten miles in the pouring rain.	A car stopped and offered him a ride.	BEFORE
10	The rain stopped.	He arrived home.	BY THE TIME
11	He lost his keys.	He couldn't open the door to his flat.	BECAUSE
12	He rang his neighbour's door bell.	All of a sudden he remembered the spare key under the doormat.	WHEN
13	His friendly neighbour made him a pot of coffee.	He only suffered from a slight hangover the next morning.	BECAUSE

1 *By the time the other guests arrived he had eaten most of the party sandwiches.*

5 Die Zukunftsformen

1 Vervollständigen Sie die Sätze mit *(to be) going to* oder *will*. Es handelt sich in diesem Gespräch über Familiengeschicke um Prognosen allgemeiner oder sicherer Art.

1 Last year my aunt bought a farm in Canada. She and her husband *are going to* leave Europe for good. Perhaps my cousin *will* join them. But he hasn't made up his mind yet.

2 My parents .... lend us some money. I've asked them and they have agreed to do so. I'm sure my grandparents .... lend us the rest when we ask them and tell them that we need the money to buy a house.

3 My brother .... help me to clear the attic. He's big and strong and I'm sure he won't mind. The only problem is that he is always so busy.

4 My sister and her family .... stay with us over the Christmas holidays. They've done so for the past few years.

5 My mother-in-law has decided to have a big birthday party. She .... invite all her children and grandchildren.

6 If you ask him, my nephew .... surely give you a lift in his car.

7 I reckon my uncle .... be mayor of our little town one day.

8 My daughter has just enrolled at university. She .... study maths and physics. I think she .... be a famous scientist one day.

9 Her in-laws .... probably look after the baby if she asks them. They live just round the corner. If they say no, she .... have to get a baby-sitter.

10 My niece is an emancipated young woman. She and her boyfriend have agreed to share the household chores. He .... do the cooking and she .... be in charge of the shopping. But they haven't decided who .... do the cleaning in their flat. I suppose they .... get someone to do it for them.

2 ***A week in the life of my boss.*** **Der Terminkalender Ihres Chefs für die kommende Woche. Erklären Sie ihm, was ihm bevorsteht. Bedienen Sie sich aus dem Verb-Pool.**

to have ✔ to have to give to meet to appear to play to give
to arrive to leave to attend

Monday	*12.30 am: lunch with the Prime Minister*
Tuesday	*10 am: psychiatrist*
	9 pm: squash with Joe
Wednesday	*10-12 am: business meeting*
	3-5 pm: university lecture: "Efficient Time Management"
	8 pm: Julia for dinner at Bellini's
Thursday	*2 pm: Live Talk Show / BBC*
Friday	*10 am: train departure to Edinburgh / 1 pm: arrival*
	3 pm: talk at the Scottish Whisky Convention
	8.30 pm: train departure / 11.30 pm: arrival London

1 On Monday at 12.30 am you *are having* lunch with the Prime Minister.
2 On Tuesday at 10 am you are having an appointment with your psychiatrist.
3 And at 9 pm you are playing squash with Joe.
4 On Wednesday you are attending a business meeting from 10 to 12 am.
5 From 3 to 5 pm you are giving a university lecture on "Efficient Time Management".
6 At 8 pm you are meeting Julia for dinner at Bellini's.
7 On Thursday you are appearing at a live Talk Show at the BBC at 2 pm.
8 On Friday at 10 am you are leaving for a business trip to Edinburgh.
9 At 3 pm you are giving a talk at the Scottish Whisky Convention.
10 At 11.30 pm you are arriving in London.

3 Termine, Termine, Termine! – einfache Gegenwart oder *ing*-Form der Gegenwart? Hier geht es um bereits festgelegte Pläne und Vereinbarungen. Achtung: Die Verben, die Sie einsetzen sollen, sind in jedem Satz in alphabetischer Reihenfolge angegeben!

	You need:
1 We are taking ……… the children to the zoo this afternoon. We'll be back at 7 o'clock. The zoo closes ……… at 6 pm, and the bus ……… an hour from the zoo to our part of town.	to close ✔ to take ✔ to take
2 We ……… to the cinema tonight. The late night performance ……… at 10 o'clock.	to go to start
3 Our friends ……… us tomorrow. Their train ……… at 5 o'clock in the afternoon.	to arrive to visit
4 My daughter ……… university this year. The summer term ……… in March and ……… in July.	to end to start to start
5 I ……… not ……… till the end of the play. My last train ……… at midnight and I mustn't miss it.	to leave to stay
6 We ……… a big party next week. It ……… father's birthday.	to be to have
7 I ……… to the dentist's next week. I ……… an appointment on Friday at 10 o'clock.	to go to have
8 We ……… tickets for the football match next week. The tickets ……… £25. They ……… very expensive.	to be to buy to cost

4 *A Blind Date.* Einfaches Futur oder Futur-Verlaufsform?

● *Linda*

▲ *Patricia*

● .... ① with us on Saturday night?
to go out / you

▲ No, I won't. I .... ② on a blind date with a guy named John. My
to go
brother arranged it. He reckons John is just my type. He thinks we
.... ③ like a house on fire.
to get on

● How .... ④ him?
to recognise / you

▲ He .... ⑤ a copy of the Financial Times in his pocket and a red
to have
rose in his hand.

● How .... ⑥ it's you?
to know / he

▲ He'll recognise me when he sees me. I .... ⑦ a bright red dress
to wear
and a big red hat.

● .... ⑧ you up at home?
to pick (up) / he

▲ No, he won't. I .... ⑨ him at the Lonely Hearts Café at 8 pm.
to meet

● What .... ⑩ all night?
to do / you

▲ We probably .... ⑪ dinner first. And later we .... ⑫
to have / to go
dancing.

● Do you think you .... ⑬ spending time with a man you've never
to enjoy
met before?

▲ Well, John .... ⑭ my tenth blind date and I'm sure I .... ⑮
to be / to have
a wonderful time on Saturday.

5 Höfliche Anfragen mit der *will*-Zukunft. Ordnen Sie den Aussagen die entsprechenden Anfragen zu und formulieren Sie sie höflich und freundlich.

open the window ✔ speak up ring for a taxi close the window sign the letter get us some tea or coffee remind me to phone the baker's excuse me send off the invitations pass on a message

1 It's absolutely stifling in this room.
Will you open the window, please?

2 It's freezing in here.
....

3 I think it's time for a drink now. We could all do with a break.
....

4 I'm afraid I couldn't hear what you just said.
....

5 It's much too late now. I've just missed the last underground.
....

6 I'm afraid I have to make a quick phone-call. I'll be back in a minute.
....

7 I urgently need to talk to the manager. It's a shame he's not in his office.
....

8 I mustn't forget to order the chocolate cake for my son's birthday party.
....

9 The secretary is going to the post-office.
....

10 The company's celebrating its 50th anniversary in June.
....

6 **„Düstere und optimistische Ausblicke in die Zukunft“. Vervollständigen Sie mit Hilfe des *Future Perfect* das Gespräch zwischen den beiden ungleichen Freundinnen kurz vor dem Jahreswechsel.**

☺ *Sandra, the optimist* ☹ *Patti, the pessimist*

☹ Next year, my husband and I *will have been* married for ten long and endless years. (to be)

☺ Next year, my husband and I .... ① ten years of joy and happiness together. (to have)

☹ Next summer, I .... ② in the same job with the same company for over seven years. (to work)

☺ Next summer, I .... ③ the pinnacle* of my career. (to reach)

☹ Statistically speaking, five years from now, the first half of my life .... ④ over. (to be)

☺ Statistically speaking, five years from now, I .... ⑤ going through my second adolescence. (to start)

☹ I'll be 35 in February. The enthusiasm of youth .... ⑥ by then. (to fade away)

☹ By the end of next year, I .... ⑦ completely grey. (to go)

☺ By the end of next year, I .... ⑧ all the colours of the rainbow. (to try)

☹ By then my husband .... ⑨ bald. (to go)

☺ By then my husband and I .... ⑩ that he looks just as sexy as Kojak. (to decide)

☹ Next year at New Year's Eve I .... ⑪ a bitter and depressed woman. (to become)

☺ No, you won't. Next year at New Year's Eve we'll be sitting here again – same time, same place.
Cheers and a Happy New Year!

* **pinnacle** the highest level of fame or success

6 Das Passiv

1 Formulieren Sie diese Küchen-Handgriffe so um, dass alle Vorgänge im Passiv beschrieben werden.

1 We serve tea in a tea pot.
Tea *is served* in a tea pot.

2 We boil potatoes in a pot.
Potatoes are boiled in a pot.

3 We prepare salads in bowls.
Salads are prepard in bowls.

4 We fry eggs in a pan.
Eggs are fried in a pan.

5 We serve coffee in cups or mugs.
Coffee is served in cups or mugs.

6 We serve wine in glasses.
Wine is served in glasses.

2 Produkte und ihre typischen Behältnisse. Ordnen Sie zunächst die Behältnisse aus dem Pool den entsprechenden Produkten zu. Formulieren Sie dann die Sätze im Passiv.

flasks ✔ jars barrels bags tubs tub tins cartons or bottles bottles crates packets

1 We sell our perfume in *flasks. Our perfume is sold in flasks.*
2 The distillery stores whisky in bottles. Whisky is stored in b.
3 But our customers buy whisky in pakd. ....
4 You fill milk in ....
5 One can buy marmalade in ....
6 We pack crisps in ....
7 We deliver bottled beer in ....
8 We distribute our catfood in ....
9 We sell chewing-gum in ....
10 We offer ice-cream in ....
11 I buy margarine in a ....

3 ***How to become rich and famous as a writer – Part One.*** **Ersetzen Sie die markierten Substantive bzw. Satzteile durch die entsprechenden Personalpronomen.**

1 The writer jots down <u>the main ideas of the story</u>.

2 He writes <u>an outline of the story</u>.

3 He fleshes out <u>the characters and the plot</u>.

4 He finishes <u>the novel</u>.

5 He sends <u>the manuscript</u> to the editor of his local newspaper.

6 The editor prints <u>excerpts</u> in the weekend edition.

7 The author offers <u>the novel</u> to a publisher.

8 If he likes it, he will publish <u>the novel</u> as a hardcover book.

9 Later, the bookshops offer <u>the paperback edition</u>.

10 The shops sell <u>50 million copies</u> in the first year.

11 Leading literary translators translate <u>the novel</u> into many languages.

4 **Formulieren Sie nun die obigen Sätze im Passiv. Verwenden Sie die Personalpronomen aus 3 als Subjekt.**

1 *They are jotted down by the writer.* ……

2 ……

3 ……

4 ……

5 ……

6 ……

7 ……

8 ……

9 ……

10 ……

11 ……

5 ***How to become rich and famous as a writer – Part Two.*** **Mit diesen Schlagzeilen verfolgt die Presse die zweite Phase Ihrer Karriere. Formulieren Sie die Sätze mit den angegebenen Konstruktionen ins Passiv Futur um.**

It is believed	1	Critics review the novel.
It is known	2	A Hollywood film producer buys the property.
It is reported	3	The producer asks the author to turn the novel into a film script.
It is understood	4	A distributor releases the film based on the novel.
It is alleged	5	Cinemagoers all over the world love the film.
It is said	6	The jury awards the Nobel prize for literature to the author.
It is understood	7	The Hollywood film producer wins the Oscar in the category Best Film Production of the Year.

1 *It is believed that the novel will be reviewed by critics.*

2 ....

....

3 ....

....

4 ....

....

5 ....

....

6 ....

....

7 ....

....

6 Welches Ereignis oder Werk gehört zu welchem Namen? Formulieren Sie diese Meilensteine der Geschichte im Passiv unter Angabe ihres „Urhebers“ und benutzen Sie die angegebenen Verben.

Shakespeare   Mary Quant   James Watt   James Cook
Sir Christopher Wren   George Gershwin ✔   Vivien Leigh
John F. Kennedy   William the Conquerer   David Lean

1 The opera 'Porgy and Bess' .... ***to compose***
2 Many famous churches and other buildings in London .... ***to design***
3 In 1066 England William .... ***to conquer***
4 The miniskirt .... ***to create***
5 The part of Scarlet O'Hara in 'Gone With The Wind' .... ***to play***
6 The films 'Lawrence of Arabia' and 'Doctor Zhivago' .... ***to direct***
7 The play 'King Lear' .... ***to write***
8 Australia and New Zealand .... ***to discover***
9 The steam engine .... ***to invent***
10 The phrase 'Ich bin ein Berliner' .... ***to coin***

1 *The opera 'Porgy and Bess' was composed by George Gershwin.*
2 ....
3 ....
4 ....
5 ....
6 ....
7 ....
8 ....
9 ....
10 ....

7 *Have you heard the latest gossip?* Hier wird der neueste Klatsch und Tratsch weitererzählt. Vervollständigen Sie die folgenden Sätze.

1 People say that Lord Sinclair was a spy for the KGB.

He is said to have been a spy for the KGB.

2 The newspapers report that his wife had a nervous breakdown when she heard about her husband's secret service activity.

She is reported ....

3 Friends of ours believe that their son regularly uses the personal services of Madame Fifi.

He is believed ....

4 I hate to be bitchy*, but have you heard about my boss? At the office it is said that his wife has left him.

She is said ....

5 They also think that she now lives with a male model twenty years younger than herself.

She is thought ....

6 My sister Dorothy knows her cosmetic surgeon. According to Dorothy, he facelifted her ten times over the past two years.

She is said ....

7 Rumour has it that she spends a fortune on clothes.

She is said ....

8 Reliable sources think that her handsome young lover will allow her to marry him because she is rolling in money.

He ....

9 Well, we all know that he had an affair with Lord Sinclair's younger daughter and that he dropped her when the other woman came along.

He ....

10 The papers report that she gave a live interview on television talking about all the details of their love life.

She ....

11 People say that she is not capable of keeping anything to herself.

She ....

I really loathe people who bitch about others, don't you?

* **bitchy** in a malicious manner

7 Die *ing*-Form als Gerundium und der Infinitiv

1 ***Our movie buff has seen a lot of films lately.*** **Suchen Sie im Diagramm Verben, die Sie dann in der *ing*-Form in die Filmtitel einsetzen. Die Namen der Hauptdarsteller helfen Ihnen bei der Zuordnung.**

1	*Missing* …………	
2	………… John Malkovich	
3	………… Down	
4	Stop ………… Sense	
5	………… the Faith	
6	She's ………… a Baby	
7	………… Rita	
8	Dirty …………	
9	………… by Numbers	
10	………… for Richard	
11	The ………… Fields	
12	………… on Heaven's Door	

<u>Starring</u>

Jack Lemmon
John Malkovich
Michael Douglas
David Byrne
Ben Stiller
Kevin Bacon
Michael Caine
Patrick Swayze
Joan Plowright
Al Pacino
Sam Waterston
Til Schweiger

A R T H O S M H G V E I J X W M S K
E S E U **M I S S** F N S E N V E R F G
E S D S E N A U A S A H B R P B E N
G L U A U B B U L S T E I G E N R E
N T C R Ö K I L L N U M F N R A K B
S C A H R N I T B M A K E H A V E I
V O T L E O E N B E N D R O W N E G
E N E O S C G D A N C E N A C H P I
N A N O U K E N E I N V I E L E E G
R Ü S K E A N P L S B I T R E N N X
Y A O S T L N K L S B X R N X T J U
S T A X J M U R S A K C R Q F S T A

2 *All the things we love doing!* Welche Satzhälften gehören zusammen? Verbinden Sie diese mit Hilfe des Gerundiums. Achtung: Gelegentlich muss auch noch eine Präposition (*in*, *of*, *on* oder *to*) eingesetzt werden!

1 I'm a real movie buff. That's why I love	a to move to the United States.
2 I study economics. Therefore I think it is worthwhile	b to read novels and short stories.
3 I like animals. Therefore I am very keen	c to go to the cinema regularly. ✔
4 I'm a keen supporter of Manchester United. That's why I enjoy	d to know more about other painting techniques.
5 I love New York City. Therefore I dream	e to hang around in cafés and meet friends.
6 I've always been a great fan of Gene Kelly and Fred Astaire. In fact, I wouldn't mind	f to go to Old Trafford to see my favourite team playing.
7 I'm a real bookworm. I like all kinds of literature but I'm particularly fond	g to try tap dancing myself.
8 One of my hobbies is water colour painting, but I'd be interested	h to support the World Wildlife Fund and similar organisations.
9 Many people say I'm something of polyglot because I'm keen	i to read the Financial Times a every day.
10 They also call me a real cosmopolitan because I always look forward	j to do nothing or to lie in bed and watch an old Hollywood movie on television.
11 I'm afraid I'm not a very active person. I really love	k to learn languages.
12 I'm a sociable person. I think it's great fun	l to organise my next trip around the world.

1 I'm a real movie buff. That's why I love *going to the cinema regularly.*

2 I study economics. Therefore I think it is worthwhile ……………………

3 I like animals. Therefore I am very keen ....

4 I'm a keen supporter of Manchester United. That's why I enjoy ....

....

5 I love New York City. Therefore I dream ....

6 I've always been a great fan of Gene Kelly and Fred Astaire. In fact, I wouldn't mind ....

7 I'm a real bookworm. I like all kinds of literature but I'm particularly fond

....

8 One of my hobbies is water colour painting, but I'd be interested ....

....

9 Many people say I'm something of a polyglot because I'm keen ....

....

10 They also call me a real cosmopolitan because I always look forward ....

....

11 I'm afraid I'm not a very active person. I like ....

12 I'm a sociable person. I think it's great fun ....

3 *A new managing director has just been appointed to solve a company crisis. This is his first speech to the board of directors.* **Was ist hier richtig: Verb + *ing*-Form oder Verb + *to*?**

Ladies and Gentlemen,

1 We can't afford .... (to spend) too much money on restructuring our company.

2 We managed .... (to improve) our corporate image. We mustn't forget .... (to improve) the quality of our products, too.

3 I'm worried because competition seems .... (to get) tougher.

4 We failed .... (to develop) a new product line.

5 Our management tends .... (to be) too optimistic.

6 We decided .... (to adopt) new marketing strategies.

7 We promised our shareholders .... (to come up) with better sales figures.

8 I suggest .... (to get) in touch with a consulting firm.

9 We even considered .... (to reduce) our workforce.

10 But we better postpone .... (to dismiss) workers. Otherwise the trade unions might threaten .... (to go) on strike. I hope .... (to be able) to solve our problems.

4 *How people change!* Beschreiben Sie, wie Ihre Freundin früher war (verwenden Sie die Konstruktion *used to* + Infinitiv) und dokumentieren Sie die Veränderungen, die sie in letzter Zeit durchgemacht hat.

1 Veronica *used to believe* (to believe) in marriage and having many children. Now she *thinks* (to think) it's much better staying single and .... (to have) a new boyfriend every month.

2 Everybody said she .... (to be) a bit of a loner because she always liked to do things on her own. But now she .... (to be) a rather sociable person.

3 She .... (to live) in the country. Now she .... (to be) a city-dweller.

4 She .... (to eat) healthy wholefood. But now she .... (to be) into fast food.

5 She .... (to love) the beautiful, unspoilt countryside. But now city life really .... (to suit) her.

6 She .... (to hate) cars. But now she .... (to drive) a fast sportscar.

7 She .... (to prefer) quiet and peaceful evenings at home. But she has become a real party animal. She .... (to enjoy) parties and likes to dance all night.

8 People .... (to call) her a country bumpkin. But now she .... (to be) considered a city-slicker because she .... (to think) she knows more about fashion and culture than country bumpkins.

8 Das Partizip

1 ***Just another ordinary day!*** **Beschreiben Sie den Tagesablauf. Beachten Sie, dass manches gleichzeitig (nebeneinander angegeben) oder nacheinander (untereinander angegeben) stattfindet.**

1	be woken up by the sound of the alarm clock get up	
2	take a shower get dressed	
3	have breakfast	watch breakfast TV
4	drive to work	listen to the news on the radio
5	work from 9 to 5 go home	
6	eat something go to the local pub	
7	drink 2 pints of beer	talk to colleagues and friends
8	come home set the alarm clock	
9	think about what happened during the day	fall asleep

1 *Having been woken up by the sound of the alarm clock, I get up.*

2 ……………………………………

3 ……………………………………

4 ……………………………………

5 ……………………………………

6 ……………………………………

7 ……………………………………

8 ……………………………………

9 ……………………………………

2 Hier finden Sie eine Ansammlung von unerfreulichen Charakteren. Bilden Sie Sätze, in denen Sie ihnen die typischen Verhaltensweisen zuordnen.

bore coward fusspot gossip narcissist ✔ pessimist scaremonger yes-man

1 He can't pass a mirror without looking into it and admiring himself, because he is such a vain person.

Being such a narcissist, he can't pass a mirror without looking into it and admiring himself.

2 Our neighbour spreads stories about burglars in our area which make us feel frightened. She likes to cause public fear.

……………………………, our neighbour spreads stories about burglars in our area which make us feel frightened.

3 The man ran away instead of helping the poor woman who was attacked by two criminals. He showed no courage whatsoever.

……………………………, the man ran away instead of helping the poor woman who was attacked by two criminals.

4 All she's interested in is buying clothes and reading fashion magazines. She doesn't seem to take an interest in anything else.

……………………………, all she's interested in is buying clothes and reading fashion magazines.

5 Grandma tends to think that horrible things are more likely to happen than good things. Sometimes she's a real prophet of doom.

……………………………, Grandma tends to think that horrible things are more likely to happen than good things.

6 My aunt loves talking about other people's private lives although it's none of her business whatsoever.

……………………………, my aunt loves talking about other people's private lives although it's none of her business whatsoever.

7 Your mother is always complaining about everything and never satisfied with anything.

……………………………, your mother is always complaining about everything and never satisfied with anything.

8 He agrees with everything other people say because he wants to please them.

...., he agrees with everything other people say.

3 *ing*-Form *(Present Participle)* oder Infinitiv? Entscheiden Sie sich nach den markierten Verben der sinnlichen Wahrnehmung für die richtige Form.

A night of horrors!

1 I was sitting in the library with my sister. First, my sister startled me. I didn't hear her *come* (to come) in. In fact, I hadn't noticed her .... (to leave) the room in the first place.

2 Then I could feel something .... (to crawl) up my leg. It was a black spider.

3 I suddenly felt someone .... (to touch) me on the shoulder. I turned round. There was nobody there. It must have been my imagination.

4 We listened to our neighbour's dog .... (to howl).

5 My sister asked me whether I had locked the door. I answered: "No, but I heard Richard .... (to lock) the door".

6 Then all of a sudden we heard a noise. Checking the living room, we watched someone .... (to climb) through the window.

7 We heard this person .... (to whisper) something.

8 Then I could smell something .... (to burn).

9 Then there was an abrupt noise and we heard someone .... (to swear) loudly. It was then that we recognized our grandad's voice. He had just lit his pipe. He was a bit drunk and had forgotten his keys. He had been trying to get into the house without waking us up.

9 Die *if*-Sätze

1 *if* oder *when*, das ist hier die Frage!

1 I'm off to the party. I hope to be back by midnight. Don't worry ...*if*... I'm late.

2 I'm afraid you can't talk to my husband right now. He's on a business trip in London. I'm sure he'll get in touch with you .... he gets back. .... there is an urgent problem, however, I can give you his mobile number.

3 I'm going shopping soon. .... you want anything, let me know. .... I'm back, we'll have a cup of coffee. But .... I'm not in by 5 o'clock I suggest you have coffee without me.

4 My brother might phone this evening. .... he does, please tell him to pick me up at the airport tomorrow.

5 .... you can spare the time, please come and see me in my office. I'd be interested in your advice on some of our new projects.

6 I'm going to London next week. .... I'm there I'll contact our British representative immediately. Mind you, ... it's not raining I might go for a long walk around Hyde Park first.

7 I suggest we leave at one o'clock. But .... you can't make it, please leave a message on my answering machine. I'll call you .... I get back.

8 I've arranged to have the company car repaired on Wednesday. I'd be very surprised .... it gets fixed* by Friday. But I'm not sure. .... you need the car, however, I'll call the garage*. .... I speak to the mechanic in charge, I'll ask .... the car will be ready for collection.

* **to fix something** to repair or mend something
* **garage** motor vehicles are repaired and serviced in a garage

2 *Ten ways to say 'No'.*

1 I really can't come to your party tomorrow evening because I have to work.
If I didn't have to work, I would come to your party.

2 Oh dear, we can't go for a walk because it looks like it's going to rain any minute.

....

3 I'm sorry, but I can't go out with you because I have this terrible headache.

....

4 I'm always so busy. That's the reason why I don't visit you very often.

....

5 No, I can't have lunch with you today because I've arranged to meet my parents.

....

6 I can't have dinner with you. You're always talking with your mouth full.

....

7 What a shame. I can't babysit for you this Saturday. I have visitors this weekend.

....

8 I'm not asking you to come upstairs for a drink because my place is in a complete mess.

....

9 I promised my girlfriend to go shopping with her. So I can't help you with your packing.

....

10 I'm not going to marry you because we're not a bit alike and have absolutely nothing in common.

....

3 *Your kind of sport?* Sie sind nicht mehr richtig fit und suchen nach einer für Sie geeigneten Sportart. Beantworten Sie die Fragen. Ordnen Sie dann der jeweiligen Sportart die entsprechenden Eigenschaften zu und fügen die Empfehlungen des Sportberaters hinzu. Richten Sie sich dabei nach Ihren Antworten.

Motor racing is your cup of tea.
Ice-hockey is the type of sport that I would recommend. ✔
You should join a rugby club or play American football.
I recommend cricket.
Tennis seems to be your kind of sport.
You should go in for horse racing or other equestrian sports.
Playing basketball or doing the highjump would be a good idea.
I recommend marathon running.
You should try paragliding or parachuting, or even hang-gliding maybe.

1 Do you like the combination of teamsports, bodychecks and ice-skating?

☒ Yes, I do. ☐ No, I don't.

If you like the combination of teamsports, bodychecks and ice-skating, ice-hockey is the type of sport that I would recommend.

☐ Yes, I do. ☒ No, I don't.

If you like the combination of teamsports, bodychecks and ice-skating, ice-hockey is not the type of sport that I would recommend.

2 Do you admire people like Boris Becker or Andre Agassi?

☐ Yes, I do. ☐ No, I don't.

3 Is altitude sickness a problem for you?

☐ Yes, it is. ☐ No, it isn't.

4 Are you very tall?

☐ Yes, I am. ☐ No, I'm not.

....

....

5 Do you like horses?

☐ Yes, I do. ☐ No, I don't.

....

....

6 Do you have good stamina and do you like long-distance running?

☐ Yes, I do. ☐ No, I don't.

....

....

7 Do you like fast cars and are you obsessed with speed?

☐ Yes, I am. ☐ No, I'm not.

....

....

8 Do you prefer team sports and games that go on for hours, if not for days on end?

☐ Yes, I do. ☐ No, I don't.

....

....

9 Do you like rough sports?

☐ Yes, I do. ☐ No, I don't.

....

....

4 *Nick Hornby's Way of Life.* Nick Hornby ist ein großer Fußballfan. Was gewesen wäre, wenn …!

1 I had absolutely no time at all. I watched television all day.

If I hadn't watched so much television, I *would have had* more time.

2 In fact, I spent the whole day in front of the television. They showed live football matches all day long.

.... so many live football matches, I .... so much time in front of the TV.

3 I didn't study for my final exams – I didn't have enough time.

.... more time, I .... harder for my final exams.

4 I didn't cover all the material that we were supposed to learn. I just didn't work hard enough.

.... harder, I .... all the material.

5 I didn't learn all the topics. As a consequence, I was nervous and panicky.

.... all the topics, I .... more confident and less nervous and panicky.

6 I didn't sleep well the night before the exam because I had terrible nightmares about failing.

.... such nightmares, I .... better.

7 During the exam, I wasn't able to concentrate. That's why I made so many mistakes.

.... to concentrate better, I .... so many mistakes.

8 In the end, I failed the exam. But I followed all the reports on the football matches.

.... all the reports, I .... the exam.

9 But I'm proud to say that I wrote a good essay on the commercial side of sports! That was only possible because I watched the entire soccer World Cup on TV.

.... the entire soccer World Cup on TV, I .... such a good essay.

10 Die unvollständigen Hilfsverben

1 Vier Möglichkeiten, „sollen“ auszudrücken. Ersetzen Sie die unterstrichenen Passagen durch Formulierungen aus 1 bis 4. Beachten Sie, dass eventuell grammatikalische Umformulierungen und Anpassungen notwendig sind!

1	2	3	4
said to (do) supposed to (do)	supposed to (do)	meant to (be) intended to (be)	was to be
rumour	arrangement	purpose	destiny

1 People say that Joe drinks three bottles of whisky every day.

Joe is said to drink three bottles of whisky every day.

2 Rumour has it that he eats ten hard-boiled eggs for breakfast.

....

3 His manager claims that he sleeps on a bed of nails.

....

4 The purpose of such torture is to gradually kill off all feelings of pain.

....

5 Some people reckon that he had robbed fifty banks when he was younger.

....

6 The reason for the bank robberies was to show the whole world that rules and regulations were not for him and that he is in a class of his own.

....

7 It is alleged that he has 30 children.

....

8 He wanted to prove that he is a real womanizer.

....

9 It is believed that he killed a lion with his bare hands.

....

10 Well, it runs in the family. People say that Joe's father Jim was a hunter in Africa and a famous bullfighter in Spain.

....

11 Jim <u>was bound to</u> become an ardent admirer of Ernest Hemingway.

....

12 And later, Jim, too, <u>became</u> the hero of many little boys – including his own son.

....

13 A film producer <u>plans</u> to do a documentary about Joe's many adventures.

....

14 <u>Rumour has it that</u> Joe will publish some of his poems next year. <u>The idea is</u> to show that he's got brains, not just brawn.

....

15 After that Joe <u>will</u> write his memoirs in order to increase his popularity.

....

16 He <u>will</u> do a promotional tour to sell the book.

....

17 <u>It was arranged that</u> this would be the start of his second career as a writer.

....

2 Entscheiden Sie bei den folgenden Sätzen, ob mit dem Verb *can* eine Fähigkeit (F) oder eine Erlaubnis (E) beschrieben wird.

	F	E	
1	☐	☐	Can you lend me some money?
2	☐	☐	Would you ask your mother whether you can lend me some money or not?
3	☐	☐	Can my brother borrow your car?
4	☐	☐	I can use your pocket calculator, can't I?
5	☐	☐	I can play the piano quite well.
6	☐	☐	I can play the piano between 3 and 6 o'clock in the afternoon.
7	☐	☐	My sister can't play tennis, but my brother is very good at it.

3 Suchen Sie nun die vier Sätze aus der vorigen Übung heraus, bei denen Sie *can* durch *may* ersetzen können.

1 ....

2 ....

3 ....

4 ....

4 *Must, mustn't, can, to be (not) allowed:* Vervollständigen Sie die Erklärungen der Verbotsschilder mit der passenden Form.

1 NO SMOKING

You might see this in the non-smoking area of a restaurant. You mustn't smoke there. You .... accept the fact that smoking cigarettes or cigars .... You .... to smoke there.

2 PLEASE DO NOT TOUCH

You might find this sign in a museum. Visitors to the museum .... look at the exhibits, but they .... to touch them.

3 NO LITTER

You might come across this sign in a picnic area. It means that you .... take all your rubbish with you. You .... leave any rubbish behind.

4 NO THOROUGHFARE. PRIVATE ROAD

This is a road sign. Vehicles .... to continue beyond this sign. They .... turn round and try a different road. Driving on ....

5 EMERGENCY EXIT ONLY

Customers might read this in a department store for example. They .... to use this exit in case of an emergency. But otherwise they .... use it. If there is no emergency, they .... try and find another exit.

6 NO CHILDREN UNDER 12

You might come across this notice at the entrance to a pub. It means that children under the age of 12 years .... enter the pub.

7 ENTER WHEN YOUR NUMBER COMES UP

That means that you .... proceed to the counter when your number appears on the screen.

8 NO DOGS

You .... bring dogs here. You might see this sign in a public garden or in a building. Exercising your dogs ....

5 All die guten Ratschläge wurden ignoriert. Jetzt kommt die Reue!

What my teacher, my parents, my friends, simply everyone always told me:

1 Work harder.

I should have worked harder.

2 Attend classes more regularly.

....

3 Don't miss so many lessons.

....

4 Do your homework every day.

....

5 Go out less.

....

6 Listen to your professor's lectures more carefully.

....

7 Don't oversleep so often.

....

8 Don't always be late for classes.

....

9 Spend the weekends studying rather than partying.

....

10 Try to avoid last year's mistakes.

....

11 Convince yourself that school isn't so bad after all.

....

If I had remembered all those things I wouldn't have failed my exam.

6 Sie haben eine Reise geplant. Es gibt an Ihrem Reiseziel einiges zu beachten. Vervollständigen Sie die Vorschriften mit *mustn't, must/have to* oder *needn't*.

1 While in the jungle, never leave your group. You mustn't walk around alone. You .... stay with your group.

2 The number-one rule is you .... drink the water. That includes tap water, ice and water from the lakes and rivers. Only drink purified boiled water. Of course you .... buy the expensive brands of bottled water, the cheaper ones will also do.

3 Only eat what our cook prepares for you. Tour members .... eat fruit or vegetables from the plants that grow in the forest.

4 Do not touch the plants. They might be poisonous. You .... pick flowers or tear off branches.

5 In order to be fit for our long walks, try going to bed early. You .... stay awake all night. But you .... go to bed at sunset.

11 Die indirekte Rede

1 Eine freudige Überraschung! Jill erfährt von ihrer Freundin Patricia, dass sie ein Baby erwartet. Natürlich muss sie diese Information sofort weitererzählen! Achten Sie auf die Änderungen, die zusätzlich zu den Anpassungen der Verbzeiten notwendig sind.

1 I have wonderful news.

Patricia told me that she had wonderful news.

2 Yesterday I had a pregnancy test done.

....

3 I am three months pregnant.

....

4 The baby is due in March next year.

....

5 I should have known myself because every morning I woke up feeling ill.

....

6 I felt sick in the mornings during the first couple of days of my pregnancy.

....

7 I gave up smoking when I found out.

....

8 I've been reading many books about how to be a good mother.

....

9 We're going away for a few days because I need a rest.

....

10 Eventually, I'm going to give up work.

....

11 You can come and babysit for me if you like.

....

2 Bei einer solchen Nachricht muss Jill sofort ihre eigenen Neuigkeiten loswerden. Und Patricia gibt selbstverständlich auch alles weiter.

1 Two months ago John asked me to marry him.

Jill said that John had asked her to marry him two months before.

2 I've been in love with him for many years now.

She said that ....

3 So I said yes.

....

4 We're getting married on 5th June.

....

5 This will be the happiest day of my life.

....

6 Will you be able to come to our wedding?

....

7 We'll spend our honeymoon on the Bahamas.

....

3 Suchen Sie im Diagramm zehn Verben, die die indirekte Rede einleiten können.

O	Z	G	S	F	M	K	H	J	T	Q	X	S	C	L
H	S	C	P	K	A	**E**	N	Z	S	T	A	T	E	Q
K	A	D	M	I	T	**X**	Z	E	A	L	D	M	A	S
G	Y	A	S	R	E	**P**	L	Y	K	R	I	E	N	T
S	V	B	N	R	L	**L**	K	H	G	E	W	E	R	T
U	S	E	X	P	L	**A**	I	N	T	M	S	A	T	R
D	R	A	S	A	M	**I**	W	E	R	A	D	D	W	E
E	Z	U	M	S	A	**N**	S	W	E	R	F	T	U	P
P	H	L	T	E	L	B	M	A	N	K	Z	U	I	O
X	W	M	N	K	X	Y	O	A	D	M	S	T	V	G
Q	S	I	M	J	Y	E	Z	U	C	A	B	S	R	N

4 Roberta trifft sich mit ihrer Kollegin Fiona in der Kantine. Es ist Fionas erster Arbeitstag nach ihrem Urlaub. Lesen Sie den Dialog.

● *Roberta*
▲ *Fiona*

● What was your holiday like?
▲ It was marvellous. We had a great time.
● Where did you go?
▲ We went to the Greek island of Rhodes.
● Who did you go with?
▲ I went with my husband.
● Where exactly did you stay?
▲ We stayed at a small hotel.
● What was the weather like?
▲ The weather was great. We had sunshine every day.
● How did you spend your time?
▲ We went for walks in the evening and did a lot of sunbathing.

5 Am Abend erzählt Roberta ihrem Mann von der Unterhaltung. Ergänzen Sie.

1 I asked her *what her holiday had been like.*
She answered that *it had been marvellous and that they had had a great time.*

2 I wanted to know ……
She answered that ……

3 I asked her ……
She replied that ……

4 I asked ……
She answered that ……

5 I wanted to know ……
She answered that ……

6 I asked her ……
She replied that ……

6 Da der Urlaub so schön war, möchten Roberta und John Fionas Urlaubsfotos ansehen. Roberta und Fiona vereinbaren telefonisch, wann sie sich treffen, und Roberta klärt während des Gesprächs mit ihrem Mann die Fragen, die Fiona stellt.

Fiona's questions:

- Are you free next Saturday?
- Is 7 pm too early?
- Would you like to have dinner at our place?
- Are you interested in last year's photographs, too?
- Will you come by car or will you take the underground?
- Do you want me to draw a map to show you how to get to our house?
- Will you bring your kids?

"John, Fiona asks …

1 *whether we are free next Saturday."*

2 ……

3 ……

4 ……

5 ……

6 ……

7 ……

7 *The party.* Jackie und Joanne erscheinen auf einer Party. Es stellt sich heraus, dass Joanne völlig falsche Vorstellungen hatte. Sie macht Jackie Vorwürfe. Ergänzen Sie den Dialog.

● *Jackie* ▲ *Joanne*

● Did you hear that? Our boss and his wife are coming to the party. How awful!

▲ But you told me *they weren't coming to the party.* You know I don't like them.

● Look, they're only serving drinks, and no food.

▲ Didn't you say …… ①. I'm starving!

- It is a fancy dress party! Everyone is wearing fancy clothes!
- ▲ I thought you said that .... ②. We're the only ones wearing normal clothes!
- There won't be any live music.
- ▲ But you said .... ③. What a shame!
- Everybody's giving presents to the hosts.
- ▲ I thought you said that .... ④. How embarrassing!

8 Verbote und Vorschriften. Im British Museum haben Sie ein Merkblatt erhalten. Zu Hause berichten Sie von diesen Vorschriften.

General Information

1. You may have to wait five or ten minutes at the entrance.
2. Queue at the end of the line.
3. Don't jump the queue.
4. Don't take bags or umbrellas into the museum rooms.
5. You needn't worry about your belongings – our cloakroom is never unattended.
6. You mustn't leave the marked path.
7. You can take photographs provided you don't use a flash.
8. You must follow the directions of our personnel.

"They gave us a leaflet which told us …

1 ....
2 ....
3 ....
4 *not to take bags and umbrellas into the museum."*
5 ....
6 ....
7 ....
8 ....

12 Der Imperativ

1 *I should have …* – Die guten Ratschläge, die nicht beachtet wurden. Schließen Sie aus den Selbstvorwürfen, welche Tipps vorangegangen sind.

1 I should have studied more. *Study more.*

2 I should have worked harder. ……………

3 I shouldn't have missed so many lessons. ……………

4 I should have done my homework every day. ……………

5 I should have gone out less. ……………

6 I should have slept in less often. ……………

7 I shouldn't have been late for classes. ……………

8 I should have tried to avoid last year's mistakes. ……………

2 Ein typischer Generationenkonflikt. Entnehmen Sie den Klagen von Thelma, was ihre Mutter wohl ständig zu ihr sagt, und verwenden Sie die angegebenen Verben.

"I am so bored. She constantly worries about my marks and wants me to spend more time doing my homework. She also doesn't want me to go out in the evenings. She even nags at me if I'm on the phone too long. If I buy make-up or lipstick, she thinks it's a waste of money. When I'm dressing up for a party, she throws me out of the bathroom because I spend ages in there. According to her, my life can't go on like this."

1 …………… more time doing your homework!

2 …………… at home in the evenings!

3 …………… on the phone so long!

4 …………… so much money on make-up and lipstick!

5 …………… of the bathroom immediately!

6 …………… your life!

get out
stay
spend **change**
chat
spend

13 Die *Phrasal Verbs*

1 Ordnen Sie dem *Phrasal Verb "look"* die richtigen Synonyme zu.

1 to look after s.o.
2 to look for s.o./s.th.
3 to look forward to s.th.
4 to look s.th. up
5 to look up

a to search for specific information
b to raise one's eyes
c to try to find s.o./s.th.
d to take care of s.o.
e to anticipate with pleasure

2 Wählen Sie aus dem obigen Pool das passende *Phrasal Verb* aus. Achten Sie auf die korrekte Zeit.

1 I've lost my glasses. Can you help me to look for them?
2 Would you mind .... our cat while we're on holiday?
3 Please, ... the word 'looks' in the dictionary.
4 I am .... to seeing my brother next week. I haven't seen him for years. I'm so glad he's coming.
5 I am .... my little sister. Have you seen her?
6 When I called his name, he .... from his newspaper.
7 She found a part-time job that allowed her to .... her old mother.

3 Wie man Dinge ein- und ausschaltet bzw. auf- und zudreht. Kreuzen Sie in der Tabelle die Verben an, die zu den Substantiven passen.

	turn on/off	switch on/off	put on/off	turn up/down
light				
television	✗	✗	✗	
water				
heating				
cooker				
volume				

4 Ersetzen Sie die markierten Verben durch ein Verb aus der Auswahl.

to put s.th. away | to put s.th. off | to put s.th. on | to put s.o. up | to put up with s.o./s.th. ✔

1 I'm afraid I can't <u>tolerate</u> this noise any more.
I'm afraid I can't <u>put up with</u> this noise any more.

2 You don't have to stay in a hotel. Our friends have offered <u>to provide accommodation for you</u>. You can use their spare room.
……………………………………………………………………………………

3 We've been <u>postponing</u> the decision about whether to buy a new car or book a trip around the world.
……………………………………………………………………………………

4 Why don't you <u>wear</u> your red dress? It looks very nice on you.
……………………………………………………………………………………

5 It's time for bed now. Pick up all your toys and <u>throw</u> them in the toy box.
……………………………………………………………………………………

5 *to get* – Setzen Sie die passende Form aus dem Pool ein.

to get up ✔ | to get out of s.th. | to get away | to get on s.th. | to get off s.th. | to get on/along with

1 She doesn't ………………… her mother-in-law. They just don't like each other.

2 Jane called to say that she has a terrible headache. I think her headache is just a way of ………………… helping us to move house.

3 We'll ………………… the bus at the next stop.

4 I start work at 7 a.m. Therefore I have to *get up* at 6 o'clock.

5 There's been so much work recently I need to ………………… for a couple of days.

6 Quick! ………………… the underground. They close the doors very fast.

14 Der Konjunktiv

1 „Schlagzeilen aus den Tagesnachrichten" – Ordnen Sie die beiden Satzhälften einander zu.

1 Environmentalists have urged that	a dividends be increased to DM 30 per share.
2 Tax authorities have recommended that	b a new runway be built at Frankfurt Airport.
3 Trade unions have suggested that	c the emission of carbon dioxide be reduced.
4 Airport authorities demanded that	d measures be taken to fight tax evasion.
5 The shareholder's association suggested that	e new job creation schemes be introduced in order to reduce the number of unemployed people.

2 Eltern-Kind-Geschichten! Setzen Sie den passenden Konjunktiv an die Stelle der unterstrichenen Passagen.

God bless them — if need be — be it right or wrong ✔ — come what may — be that as it may

1 My parents, <u>who are such wonderful people and I wish them all the best</u>, said they'll always stand by me.

My parents, ……………………, said they'll always stand by me.

2 <u>Whatever happens</u>, I can rely on them. ……………………, I can rely on them.

3 <u>Even if this is so</u>, I have to try and stand on my own two feet.

……………………, I have to try and stand on my own two feet.

4 <u>Whether it's right or wrong</u>, I'm moving out. *Be it right or wrong,* I'm moving out.

5 <u>If necessary</u>, I can always move back home. ……………………, I can always move back home.

15 Frageform und Verneinung

1 Stellen Sie die passenden Fragen, indem Sie die Verben einsetzen.

1 I'm looking for my little sister. → Who *are you looking* for?

2 I'm looking for my little sister's teddy bear. → What .... for?

3 She was playing with her friend. → Who .... with?

4 He comes from Manchester. → Where .... from?

5 He lives in the posh part of town. → Which part of town .... in?

6 I am laughing at your jokes. → What .... at?

7 This coat is made of real Harris tweed. → What .... this coat .... of?

8 We were talking about our problems. → What .... about?

2 Phil ist ein sehr guter Schüler. Sein Zwillingsbruder David ist allerdings das genaue Gegenteil! Geben Sie an, wie die lange bzw. die kurze verneinte Form der verwendeten Verben aussieht!

Phil ☺	David ☹
1 <u>is</u> a very good student.	*is not* / *isn't*
2 <u>has made</u> good progress in his studies.	.... / ....
3 <u>does</u> his homework right after school.	.... / ....
4 <u>can</u> answer difficult questions.	.... / ....
5 <u>learns</u> fast.	.... / ....
6 <u>seems</u> to be doing well in all subjects.	.... / ....
7 <u>speaks</u> English very well.	.... / ....
8 <u>is</u> going to study a second language next year.	.... / ....
9 <u>will</u> pass his final exams.	.... / ....

3 *Talking about the weather.* Bilden Sie die passenden Fragen.

1 Yes, I think it's going to snow.
Do you think it's going to snow?

2 No, it wasn't raining last night.
....

3 Yes, indeed, it snowed three years ago on 1st November.
....

4 The weather turned dull a few days ago.
....

5 Yes, I think it's going to stop raining.
....

4 Ergänzen Sie die notwendigen *Question Tags* für das folgende freundliche Gespräch in einem Restaurant.

● *Phoebe* ▲ *Michael*

● Gosh, look at the prices! This has become a very expensive restaurant, *hasn't it?*

▲ Do you really think so. It isn't that expensive, ... ①?

● The girl sitting at the table by the window doesn't know you by any chance, ... ②? She's been staring at you for the past ten minutes now.

▲ I don't think we know each other. You're not jealous, ... ③?

● Dear me, no. Do you remember, we used to come here for lunch, ... ④?

▲ Yes, I remember. There is another very good Indian restaurant round the corner, ... ⑤? But I think you'd rather stay here, ... ⑥?

● Yes, I'd rather stay here. You wouldn't really expect such an excellent restaurant in this part of town, ... ⑦? Oh, look, they serve oysters here. You like oysters, ... ⑧?

▲ Yes, I do. Let's order, ... ⑨?

16 Der unbestimmte Artikel

1 *a* oder *an*?

1 The price for petrol is five dollars ..a.. gallon. That is too much. What .... rip-off!

2 You're allowed to drive through these villages at 10 kilometres .... hour.

That's .... rather slow pace, isn't it?

3 What .... beautiful summer's day! It is .... pity that I have to work.

I'd much rather go for .... walk.

4 I go to the dentist's at least ten times .... year. He is such .... handsome young man. That's why.

5 Take .... seat, please. You might have to wait for half .... hour.

6 I have such .... headache. I think I'll take .... aspirin.

7 He's .... Englishman. He has .... strange sense of humour and is slightly eccentric.

2 Setzen Sie den unbestimmten Artikel ein, falls erforderlich.

1 Mr Smith is ..a.. leading local businessman. Last month he was elected .... President of the Greenwich Golf Club for the third time.

2 My parents are lawyers, but I don't want to be .... lawyer.

3 As .... Chairman of Microsoft Inc., Bill Gates is one in the most successful managers of the world.

4 As .... British Prime Minister you live and work in Number 10, Downing Street.

5 He was appointed .... chief economist at the Bank of England in 1998.

6 He was made .... captain of the national soccer team.

7 Richard Burton was considered to be .... excellent actor. He was nominated .... Best Actor in 1969.

8 He went to the fancy dress party dressed as .... policeman.

3 „Ein passender Ausruf für verschiedene Situationen“ – Vervollständigen Sie – wo nötig – die Sätze mit dem unbestimmten Artikel.

What .... beautiful morning!	What .... fool I've been!	What .... luck! ✔
What .... terrible weather!	What .... good idea!	What .... man!
What .... rotten luck!	What .... beautiful scenery!	
What .... fantastic view!	What .... genius he is!	

4 Ordnen Sie nun die Ausrufe den passenden Szenen zu.

1 We thought we'd missed the plane because our train to the airport was thirty minutes late. But our plane was delayed one hour because of bad weather conditions. We all said: *What luck!*

2 He broke his arm on the first day of his holiday. All his friends said: ....

3 When I got up at 7 o'clock I opened the window. The sun was shining and the sky was blue. I said: ....

4 The mountaineers had reached the peak and were admiring the breath-takingly beautiful mountain range. They could see a long way. They exclaimed: ....

5 Then unfortunately it started pouring with rain. They said: ....

6 I decided not to marry him because he didn't have enough money. Today he's a millionaire. Serves me right. ....

7 Two years ago John had a great idea for a new type of dishwasher. Last year he invented a novel type of lawnmower. He is so clever. ....

8 Yesterday we took the kids to the cinema to see the latest Tom Cruise film. After the performance the girls went: Ah, ...

9 Last year we spent our summer holidays travelling through Scotland. The countryside is so stunning. We kept saying: ....

10 "What about a trip to the seaside?" my boyfriend suggested. I love the sea so I replied: ....

17 Der bestimmte Artikel

1 Ordnen Sie den folgenden Formulierungen, die ohne den bestimmten Artikel gebildet werden, die einzig richtige Bedeutung zu.

1 to go to bed	a to do a job and earn one's living
2 to go to school	b to sleep
3 to go to hospital	c to study for an academic degree
4 to go to work	d to serve a jail sentence for a criminal offence
5 to go to prison	e to be educated and taught by teachers
6 to go to court	f to go to a religious service
7 to go to university	g to undergo an operation
8 to go to church	i to fight a legal case

2 Mit oder ohne bestimmten Artikel? Setzen Sie die Substantive entsprechend ein. Orientieren Sie sich an den Formulierungen aus 1.

1 Grandma is a very religious person. She goes to *church* every Sunday.

2 When I was ill all my colleagues came to .... to visit me.

3 My friend, who is a surgeon, works at ....

4 After leaving ...., I travelled around the world. I didn't want to start .... immediately.

5 The injured woman was taken to ....

6 A group of tourists went to .... to look at the famous frescoes depicting biblical scenes.

7 Mr Smith was sent to .... to serve a 5-year jail sentence for robbery.

8 I'm not going out tonight. I need my beauty sleep. I want to go to .... early.

9 If I pass my A-levels I'll go to .... to study law.

10 I was at .... yesterday to meet my daughter's teacher.

3 Suchen Sie im Diagramm die Namen von neun Instrumenten bzw. Berufsbezeichnungen aus der Musikwelt.

A	S	F	M	A	I	Z	T	J	G	C	M	B	A	V	S	Q	R
H	T	E	H	J	K	P	I	L	I	H	L	H	G	D	M	M	L
K	B	N	A	U	I	I	L	O	P	E	D	R	U	M	S	J	H
B	W	Q	C	V	Y	A	N	**G**	B	K	U	L	D	V	A	H	L
A	R	C	U	S	J	N	I	**U**	A	U	T	P	O	I	X	L	V
M	A	R	A	V	I	O	L	**I**	N	I	O	P	M	O	O	S	C
G	I	T	A	B	N	M	L	**T**	D	T	T	R	U	M	P	E	T
Q	A	E	G	N	H	J	L	**A**	L	R	W	B	M	S	H	L	H
A	C	O	M	P	O	S	E	**R**	E	P	O	E	S	P	O	L	W
D	T	Z	J	A	M	O	N	J	A	C	L	A	R	I	N	E	T
G	O	E	R	T	Z	J	L	A	D	F	S	X	J	A	E	L	P
B	U	Z	T	R	E	V	A	B	E	C	R	K	I	N	D	J	H
D	R	A	M	T	N	D	E	R	R	U	H	U	F	O	Q	A	T

4 Ordnen Sie die gefundenen Begriffe den angegebenen Persönlichkeiten zu. Vergessen Sie nicht, gegebenenfalls den bestimmten Artikel zu ergänzen!

1 Jimmy Hendrix played *the guitar*.

2 I've been looking forward to a recording with B. B. King on .... and Eric Clapton on ....

3 Chet Baker, Dizzy Gillespie and Louis Armstrong played ....

4 Duke Ellington played ....

5 Benny Goodman played ....

6 Charlie Parker played ....

7 Yehudi Menuhin played ....

8 Billy Cobham plays ....

9 Glenn Miller was one of .... world's most famous ....

10 .... Cole Porter is famous for his contribution to .... world of musicals.

5 *Some interesting facts about famous musicians.* Setzen Sie, falls erforderlich, den bestimmten oder unbestimmten Artikel ein!

1 Eric Clapton plays the guitar. He's .... Englishman living in .... south of England.

2 Charlie Parker played .... saxophone. He is considered .... creator of .... famous Bebop style. He is widely acknowledged as .... master of .... jazz music.

3 Louis Armstrong was born in Louisiana. He was married to .... well-known singer Ella Fitzgerald.

4 Ringo Starr played .... drums for .... Beatles. When .... band split up he started .... solo career.

5 Glenn Miller is .... composer of .... lot of evergreen songs. He played all over .... world. He founded .... era of .... Swing. On .... flight to Paris, his plane disappeared.

6 Stevie Wonder plays .... piano. He is one of .... most successful contemporary musicians.

6 Mit oder ohne bestimmten Artikel? Vervollständigen Sie die Wegbeschreibungen.

1 How do I get to .... Paddington Station, please?

2 Take .... bus. There is a bus stop round .... corner.

3 And how do I get to .... British Museum, please?

4 Well, I suggest going by .... underground.

5 Get off at .... Russell Square and walk to .... museum.

6 When you see .... big sign saying “British Museum”, you're almost there.

7 If you don't want to take .... underground, you can go on .... foot.

18 Das Substantiv – die Pluralbildung

1 Zunächst als Einstieg ein Kreuzworträtsel: Welche Substantive sind von den folgenden Adjektiven abgeleitet und umgekehrt?

1 strong
2 patient
3 advantageous
4 mysterious
5 proud
6 sarcastic
7 truth
8 generosity
9 energy
10 ambition
11 length

Das Lösungswort ist das Adjektiv: ....

Das entsprechende Substantiv lautet: ....

2 Die Bildung des Plurals – Ordnen Sie die angegebenen Substantive in die richtige Spalte ein.

computer bus car ✔ bicycle fax hobby report mystery
pass disk company ✔ desk telephone paper toy meeting
colleague break office chair cupboard boss ✔ pencil play

-s		-es	y > ies
cars	....	*bosses*	*companies*
....	....	....	....
....	....	....	....
....	....	....	....

3 *The rule and exceptions to the rule.* Gewohnheiten und die Ausnahmen von der Regel.

1 Normally, I buy one newspaper on my way to work. But when something important happens I buy two or more newspapers.

2 Usually, I eat one kilo of apples per day. But when my sister comes to visit me, I get two .... because she always brings her children. They are crazy about apples.

3 I used to invite my colleagues to dinner once a month. My wife likes to cook exotic meals. But last time my colleagues brought their ...., too, and they started a big discussion about emancipation and women's rights.

4 On Saturdays I always buy one loaf of bread. I eat one half over the weekend, the other half lasts me until the next weekend. But if I go on one of my trips to the mountains I need three .... of bread which make six ....

5 I think everyone needs a hobby. I have four ....: I love reading, going to the cinema, swimming and cycling.

6 In winter I have to wear a scarf. If I don't, I catch a cold immediately. On extremely cold days I even put on two or three .... just to be on the safe side.

7 My mother always has a photo of her family with her. When she meets up with her best friend, however, she usually shows her at least forty or fifty of the latest .... of her grandchildren.

8 I can't eat more than one potato: when I was a child, my mother was very fond of .... and served them with absolutely everything.

9 One thing I like about big cities is that the markets offer every type of fruit or vegetable throughout the year. Ever since I had mango and avocado salad at my brother's place, I go and buy .... and .... at least once a month.

19 Das Substantiv – der Genitiv

1 Kreuzen Sie im Diagramm an, aufgrund welcher Regel der in den Beispielsätzen enthaltene Genitiv gebildet wurde.

		1	2	3	4	5	6	7	8	9	10
s-Genitiv	Personen										
	Tiere										
	Orte, Länder										
	Zeitangaben				✘						
of-Genitiv	Dinge										
	Abstrakta										

1 These are children's books.

2 The cat's name is Felix.

3 May I have a glass of milk.

4 In a week's time we'll be in London. ✔

5 Let's have an hour's rest.

6 The effect of the ozone hole will be disastrous.

7 This is my boss's desk.

8 There is a bird's nest in the garden.

9 Germany's export figures are not as good as they used to be.

10 The door of our house is open.

2 Kreuzen Sie an, wie der Genitiv zu bilden wäre, wenn man die beiden angegebenen Substantive verbinden würde.

				's	of
1	the Queen	....	visit to Berlin	☐	☐
2	environment	....	protection	☐	☐
3	this year	....	crop	☐	☐

4 my aunt	....	birthday	☐	☐
5 science	....	progress	☐	☐
6 football match	....	result	☐	☐
7 everybody	....	darling	☐	☐
8 children	....	toys	☐	☐
9 my dog	....	name	☐	☐

3 Suchen Sie aus dem Diagramm sieben Berufe heraus, aus denen Sie dann den Namen des entsprechenden Geschäftes bilden.

W	B	O	J	**S**	K	L	E	B	N	I	Z	K	F	E
D	U	G	E	**T**	Z	T	D	E	N	T	I	S	T	B
F	T	E	Z	**A**	L	K	J	K	J	W	R	I	B	M
U	C	J	K	**T**	L	O	T	I	E	W	H	A	A	N
C	H	E	M	**I**	S	T	P	O	I	E	F	W	K	B
A	E	J	C	**O**	N	F	E	C	T	I	O	N	E	R
E	R	O	P	**N**	A	F	Z	U	C	I	N	P	R	O
S	J	G	R	**E**	E	N	G	R	O	C	E	R	Y	N
Y	Q	W	B	**R**	T	R	L	F	I	E	G	E	G	V

4 Setzen Sie nun den Namen des Geschäfts in den passenden Satz ein!

1 I bought a writing pad and two pencils at the *stationer's*.

2 Go and get us ten sausages from the ....

3 There is a .... just round the corner. I'll get us some bread for breakfast.

4 I have an appointment at the .... today. I've got a terrible toothache.

5 Would you mind getting us some fresh vegetables and fruit from the

.....................?

6 I've got such a headache and I've run out of aspirins. I better go to the

.... and buy some.

7 Why don't you go to the .... and buy your friend a box of chocolates for her birthday.

5 Welcher Kontext gehört zu welcher Schlagzeile?

"Newton's discovery" ....

"The discovery of Newton" ....

A Sir Isaac Newton discovered the law of gravitation.
Analysing the incident of an apple falling on his head, he found out that the gravitation constant equals the acceleration per second that a mass of one gram causes at a distance of one centimetre.

B Britain rediscovers one of the country's most famous scientists. A new biography showing many new facets of this extraordinary man will be published next week.

6 Genitive der schwierigeren Art – Setzen Sie die angegebenen Substantive im Genitiv in die Sätze ein. In manchen Fällen gibt es zwei Lösungen! Welche sind es?

1	I don't like your *friends'* attitude.	**friends**
2	I can't stand the .... secretary.	**boss**
3	Our .... secretaries are rather nice.	**bosses**
4	The .... bowls need to be cleaned.	**cats**
5	This is .... new cottage.	**Mr and Mrs Jones**
6	The .... toys are in the big box on the top shelf.	**kids**
7	The .... safety standards need to be improved.	**airlines**
8	.... daughter is our new neighbour.	**Mr Evans**
9	It's the .... twentieth wedding anniversary next week.	**Millers**
10	I'm driving my .... car.	**parents**

7 „Die liebe Verwandtschaft …“ – einfacher und doppelter Genitiv? Vervollständigen Sie außerdem die Genitiv-Formen und tragen Sie aus dem Pool das beschriebene Verwandtschaftsverhältnis ein.

son ✔ father husband cousin brother sister-in-law in-laws

1 Jack is a son of my mother's sister. He is my cousin.

2 My nephew .... is my brother John. A sister .... – well, that's me, of course.

3 One of the six daughters of Grandma .... and Grandpa .... is Aunt Jane. Her .... is my Uncle James. He's Jack .... father. Remember, Jack is a ....

4 Joe is a .... of John .... and of course also a brother .... He's getting married to Joanne. She is my dentist and a good friend of Aunt Jane .... So next time I go to the dentist ...., I actually go and see my .... My brother's .... are our dentist .... mother and father. Isn't that funny?

8 *of* oder *'s*?

1 .... (whiskies / Scotland) are famous. .... (the beauty / the hills and lakes) also attracts many tourists.

2 Where have you put .... (TV guide / this week)? I'd like to see what's on telly tonight.

3 We've done .... (work / a hard day). Let's call it a day now and go home.

4 I'm so exhausted. I think I need .... (holiday / a week).

5 We must try to improve .... (the quality / our products). .... (sales figures / this year) don't look rosy.

6 He is .... (youngest Prime Minister / Britain). .... (the number / votes) he gained is the highest in post-war Britain.

20 Das Substantiv – die Großschreibung

1 Ordnen Sie den Anlässen das korrekte Datum zu.

1 Valentine's Day	f	a	1st January
2 Thanksgiving Day	....	b	4th July
3 Halloween	....	c	31st December
4 New Year's Day	....	d	fourth Thursday in November
5 April Fool's Day	....	e	25th December
6 Boxing Day	....	f	14th February
7 Independence Day	....	g	1st April
8 New Year's Eve	....	h	31st October
9 Christmas Day	....	i	26th December

2 Vervollständigen Sie die Definitionen mit dem „besonderen Tag".

1 At ...., people dress up as witches and wear scary masks.

2 .... is a holiday in the United States, celebrating the survival of early English travellers to America, who nearly died of hunger. The traditional meal served on .... is turkey.

3 The third day celebrating Christmas is called ....

4 .... marks the national day in the United States, celebrating the signing of the Declaration of Independence in 1776.

5 On *Valentine's Day* people send cards or give presents to someone they love.

6 .... marks the beginning of a new year.

7 .... is the day before New Year's Day. People have parties to celebrate the New Year.

8 On .... people play tricks on each other.

9 .... follows Christmas Eve and precedes Boxing Day.

3 Vervollständigen Sie die Sätze, indem Sie die fehlenden Anfangsbuchstaben ergänzen. Achten Sie auf Groß- und Kleinschreibung!

1 The u/ U nited n/ N ations o/ O rganisation is headquartered in n/...... ew y/...... ork c/...... ity. It is probably one of the most important o/ o rganisations where most n/ n ations are represented.

2 The f/...... ederal b/...... ureau of i/...... nvestigation is an i/...... nstitution for the i/...... nvestigation of criminal cases that concern more than one s/...... tate of the USA.

3 The origin of the u/...... nited s/...... tates of a/...... merica lies in the c/...... onstitution: today 53 s/...... tates form part of the USA.

4 w/...... all s/...... treet is a collective term for the leading financial centre in the u/...... nited s/...... tates. But of course it also simply denotes the name of a s/...... treet in l/...... ower m/...... anhattan.

5 The r/...... ocky m/...... ountains are one of the most beautiful m/...... ountain ranges in the world.

6 In good t/...... imes, if my f/...... inancial situation is good, I enjoy reading the f/...... inancial t/...... imes. If I'm out of cash, however, I never read or talk about f/...... inancial business.

7 The b/...... ank of e/...... ngland is not an ordinary b/...... ank. It is the c/...... entral b/...... ank of the u/...... nited k/...... ingdom.

8 This year, the s/...... cottish w/...... hiskey c/...... onvention takes place in the s/...... cottish town of Edinburgh. All important w/...... hiskey d/...... istilleries will attend it.

9 The b/...... ritish p/...... rime m/...... inister lives and works in 10, d/...... owning s/...... treet in l/...... ondon. One of the most fascinating sights in l/...... ondon is the t/...... ower of l/...... ondon. It is a building which actually consists of more than one t/...... ower. In the m/...... iddle a/...... ges it was used as a prison. In our day and a/...... ge, however, people would never accept a prison in the c/...... entre of a big c/...... ity.

21 Die Personalpronomen

1 „Geben und nehmen!“ – Ersetzen Sie die unterstrichenen Passagen durch Personalpronomen und verwenden Sie *to* bzw. *for*.

1 I bought my little brother a football.
I bought it for him.

2 We sold our neighbours our van for $100.

3 Could your brother fetch me the glasses, please?

4 Get your mother a nice cup of tea, will you?

5 The shop sells home-made sandwiches to you and your employees, doesn't it?

6 Could you pass the salt to your father?

7 I gave twenty copies of the dictionary to your secretary Ms Adams.

8 Have your translators received the dictionaries?

2 Bilden Sie, ausgehend von den genannten Vorschlägen und Anweisungen, den Imperativ und verwenden Sie die richtigen Pronomen.

1 Why don't you take off your jacket? *Take it off!*

2 Please hang up your coats on the coat rack over there.

3 I'm afraid we have to put off the meeting until tomorrow.

4 Don't throw away last year's business reports.

5 I'd like to try on these dresses.

22 Die Possessivpronomen

1 „Besitztümer" – Ergänzen Sie das adjektivische *(my, your)* oder das substantivische *(mine, yours)* Possessivpronomen.

1 Windsor Castle belongs to the Queen and the Royal Family, doesn't it? Yes, it is *their* castle. It has been *theirs* for many decades.

2 Will all ferry passengers please make sure that they take all .... personal possessions with them.

3 When .... uncle dies, you'll come into possession of a great deal of property. Everything will be .... He has no son. You're the rightful heir to .... entire fortune.

4 Does the Chase Manhattan Bank in New York City still belong to the Rockefellers? Yes, it's still .... owners are the Rockefellers.

5 My brother and I will inherit the house when .... parents die. It will be ....

6 My sister bought a plot of land in Scotland. 600 acres of good farmland are .... boyfriend will join her next year.

7 During the Great Depression in the 1920s everyone tried to be rid of .... bank notes and coins and invested in material assets.

2 Setzen Sie die entsprechenden Possessivpronomen in die Lücken ein.

1 Oh dear! I think I've lost my pen. May I borrow one of ...., please?

2 By the way, tell your sister that we need her colour pencils, and you better bring ...., too, just in case she forgets to bring ....

3 I hope the others don't turn up without their watercolours. I'll bring .... at any rate. However, ... are better-quality colours.

4 Oh! And Tom, do remind your brother to bring the pen that I lent him. He had lost ...., you see. And I gave him .... because I didn't need a pen at the time.

23 Die Reflexivpronomen

1 ***Mother's wonderful pearls of wisdom.* „Die Lebensweisheiten einer Mutter" – Entscheiden Sie sich zunächst für das korrekte Verb aus dem Pool – sie sind alle reflexiv zu verwenden! Setzen Sie dann noch die erforderlichen Reflexivpronomen ein.**

treat ✔ control defend make a fool of look after pay for make cut burn hate enjoy blame behave

1. After a hard day's work, you deserve something good. So *treat yourself* to something nice.
2. We must never rely too much on other people taking care of us. We should all ....
3. If someone treats you unfairly, or unjustly accuses you of something, don't give in. Make sure you ....
4. When you're dating a man for the first time, don't let him pay the bill. Tell him: "I'd rather ...."
5. When you're working in the kitchen, be very careful with knives. Don't .... And mind the grill. You might ....
6. When you and your friends go to a party, have a good time and .... But be careful! Don't eat or drink too much. Make sure you always .... There is nothing worse than being drunk or sick at a party.
7. Tell your children to mind their manners and to .... when they go to their friends' houses.
8. If you say or do something stupid, don't worry. We all .... sometimes. You live and learn.
9. But if you make a serious mistake, don't say it's someone else's fault. ....
10. When you're having friends over for dinner tell them to feel at home and .... comfortable.

24 Die Demonstrativpronomen und -adjektive

1 Stecken Sie die Beispielsätze in die richtige „Schublade“.

This / these …	That / those …
1 kündigen eine Sache an, die anschließend genannt oder beschrieben wird. 3 beschreiben etwas zeitlich Näherliegendes. 5 beschreiben etwas örtlich Näherliegendes.	2 kommentieren oder schließen etwas bereits Genanntes oder Beschriebenes ab. 4 beschreiben etwas zeitlich Entferntes. 6 beschreiben etwas örtlich Entferntes. 7 betonen eine Abneigung oder Schwärmerei.

☐ 1 "… and they lived happily ever after." Those words mark the traditional ending of a fairy tale.

☐ 2 This is what to do to get rid of a hiccup – jump up and down and count to five while holding your breath.

☐ 3 Paul Newman is my favourite male actor. I just adore those wonderful blue eyes of his.

☐ 4 These magazines here on my desk must be yours.

☐ 5 We could spend our holidays on one of those little islands in the South Sea.

☐ 6 We better solve these computer problems before we continue our work.

☐ 7 Those days when we used typewriters instead of computers are gone, thank God.

2 Ergänzen Sie nun *that/those* oder *this/these*.

1 Can you sign .... form here for me, please?

2 I love .... old black and white Hollywood movies, don't you?

3 Now stop interfering. ....'s none of your business.

4 .... were the days! The pace of life was not as hectic as it is now.

5 .... delivery problem is nothing compared to all .... difficulties with our suppliers that we had last year.

6 .... is exactly what he just said.

25 Die Relativpronomen und Relativsätze

1 Geben Sie für jeden Satz an, in welche der drei Kategorie er gehört.

1	2	3
Relativsätze bezogen auf Personen	Relativsätze bezogen auf Dinge	Relativsätze bezogen auf Sachverhalte (Satzteile)

1 The man who lives next door never says a word. ☐
2 We often go to London for the day, which is very nice. ☐
3 The train to London, which leaves every hour, is a fast train. ☐
4 I like living near London, which is the most exciting city in the world. ☐
5 Our new neighbour won't come to our dinner party, which is a pity. ☐
6 My father, who loves trains, used to work for a railway company. ☐
7 We live in a house which is very old. ☐

2 Welche Erklärung passt zu welchem Relativsatz?

1	2
The scientists, who know about the dangers of genetic engineering, call for a ban on genetically manipulated food.	The scientists who know about the dangers of genetic engineering call for a ban on genetically manipulated food.

A All scientists are aware of the dangerous effects of genetic engineering and therefore want a ban on genetically manipulated food.

B Only the scientists who know about this threat call for a ban. Other scientists don't support their colleagues' call for a ban on genetically manipulated food.

3 *The world of fashion.* Die definierten Begriffe in der rechten Spalte sind durcheinander geraten. Ordnen Sie sie der richtigen Definition zu und vervollständigen Sie diese mit den Relativpronomen.

1 *A model* is a person *who* wears clothes .... are photographed or shown to potential buyers.

2 .... is a walkway .... models walk along presenting new clothes to an audience.

3 .... is a person .... creates clothes.

4 .... is a country .... many fashion houses have their headquarters. and .... is famous for its haute couture.

5 .... is an event .... is organized by fashion designers to present their latest creations.

6 .... is a set of clothes and accessoires .... are designed for the new season.

7 .... is fashion .... is mass-produced and can be bought off-the-peg.

8 .... is a time .... all the famous fashion houses present their new collections.

catwalk
fashion designer
France
fashion week
collection
fashion
fashion show
model ✔
ready-to-wear

4 Formen Sie die Sätze so um, dass die Reaktionen der Umwelt auf die Ereignisse als Relativsatz wiedergegeben werden.

1 Yesterday our neighbours were killed in a plane crash. The entire neighbourhood was shocked.

Yesterday our neighbours were killed in a plane crash, *which shocked the entire neighbourhood.*

2 People are always pushing and shoving in the underground. I find this very annoying.

People are always pushing and shoving in the underground, ...

....

3 Yesterday one of my colleagues shut the door in my face. That was very rude of him.

Yesterday one of my colleagues shut the door in my face, ...

....

4 Manchester United were the better team, but the match was decided on penalties. Leeds won. It was most unfair.

Leeds won, ...

....

5 The athlete had failed to qualify for the Olympic Games by one hundredth of a second. Everyone thought it was such a pity.

She had failed to qualify for the Olympic Games by one hundredth of a second, ...

....

5 „Schreckliche Zeitungsmeldungen" – Verbinden Sie beide Sätze mit Hilfe von *which* und *who*. Achten Sie auf den Unterschied zwischen entbehrlichen und unentbehrlichen Informationen und setzen Sie entsprechend die Kommata.

1 A UN environmental group warned that eating fish poses a health hazard. The fish is caught in polluted rivers and lakes.

A UN environmental group warned that eating fish which is caught in polluted rivers and lakes poses a health hazard.

2 Greenpeace called on all governments to issue warnings to consumers. Greenpeace is an organization for the protection of the environment.

....

3 We grieve the death of a child. The child was killed by a pit bull terrier.

....

4 60 million land mines are still scattered around the world. They kill up to 10 people every day.

....

5 A huge oil spill blackened 60 kilometres of coastline in Brazil. The oil spill killed thousands of fish and birds.

....

6 Brazil's oil spill was caused when 4 million litres of oil escaped from a burst pipeline. It was the worst spill in 25 years.

....

6 „Noch mehr schlechte Nachrichten!" – Verbinden Sie erneut die beiden Sätze mit *which* oder *who*. Achten Sie darauf, dass sich der Relativsatz auch hier auf ganze Satzteile und nicht nur auf Substantive beziehen kann.

1 A plane crashed into a residential neighbourhood near Bombay. This led to the killing of 60 people on board and 6 others on the ground.

A plane crashed into a residential neighbourhood near Bombay, which led to the killing of 60 people on board and 6 others on the ground.

2 An investigation is still underway. It will determine the cause of the accident.

....

3 The crash has raised questions about the safety procedures for India's planes. They are sometimes called coffins in the air because of their bad record. ....

....

4 In 1986 Swedish technicians recorded levels of radiation. This was the beginning of the worst crisis in the history of nuclear power plants. ....

....

5 Fourteen years after the worst radiation accident in history, the remaining working reactor will be closed. The accident had taken place at the Chernobyl power station. ....

....

26 Die unbestimmten Pronomen (*some, any, much, many,* usw.)

1 Formulieren Sie anhand der folgenden Stichpunkte Fragen, die Sie bei einem Vorstellungsgespräch dem Personalchef der Firma stellen. Verwenden Sie entweder *how much* oder *how many*.

1 people – your company – to employ

How many people does your company employ?

2 money – secretaries – to earn per month

....

3 hours per day – employees – to work

....

4 time – workers – to have for their lunch breaks

....

5 holidays per year – they – to be entitled to

....

6 flexibility – you – to allow your workers

....

2 *Profiles.* Beschreiben Sie die verschiedenen Typen, indem Sie *much, few, little, a lot of* ergänzen.

A quiet person ... doesn't talk *much.*

... speaks only a .... ① words at a time.

... communicates very .... ② with other people.

A lonely person There are very .... ③ people around him.

He has .... ④ friends and doesn't go out

.... ⑤.

A sociable person ... knows .... ⑥ people.

... misses out .... ⑦ parties.

3 Vervollständigen Sie die angegebenen Informationen sinngemäß! Sie brauchen *much, many, few* und *little*.

1 There was a food shortage after the drought. There was .... food left. There wasn't .... food available.

2 There are not enough hospitals in third world countries. There are very .... doctors.

3 There is a lack of unspoilt countryside on our planet. There is very .... unspoilt countryside to be found.

4 There are not enough jobs relative to the number of job seekers. There are too .... jobs available, there aren't .... jobs.

5 We've almost run out of time to solve the world's environmental problems. We've got .... time left. In other words we haven't got .... time to spare.

6 The resources which poor countries have in order to finance development projects are not sufficient. They have .... resources.

7 Some highly indebted countries are almost broke. The have .... money, or, in other words, they don't have .... money.

4 *Leisure activities.* Ein ungleiches Paar – was die Freizeitaktivitäten anbelangt. Vervollständigen Sie die Beschreibung mit *much, many* und *a lot (of)*.

1 My boyfriend and I do *a lot of* travelling. We've visited so .... interesting countries on our trips abroad.

2 I am very fond of the mountains. I do .... mountain-climbing. But my boyfriend reckons that there isn't .... else to do.

3 He loves the sea and therefore does .... swimming. I don't like it .... myself, to be quite honest.

4 He gets .... pleasure out of water-skiing and sailing, too. There are so .... water sports activities, he claims. Well, the only one that I care for .... is fishing.

5 At home I spend .... my time going to the cinema. My boyfriend thinks there are too .... boring films, and going to the cinema is a waste of time.

6 I'm also crazy about dancing and so I go to discos .... My boyfriend wouldn't be seen dead in a disco. According to him there are too .... people and too .... noise, and he doesn't like crowded and noisy places.

7 We don't have .... in common. But we try and spend as .... time together as possible. After all, we very .... enjoy each other's company.

5 Sie erzählen von der gestrigen Besprechung. Sie war leider nicht – wie in der Vorlage – ein Erfolg, sondern ein Flop. Verneinen Sie die Sätze.

1 Yesterday's meeting was a big success. There were some questions we wanted them to answer if possible.

Yesterday's meeting was a disaster. There weren't any questions we wanted them to answer.

2 They had some time left to explain everything in detail.

....

3 The managing director told us some interesting facts about the project.

....

4 I had read some of their reports.

....

5 I asked for some additional information about your company.

....

6 Luckily, they didn't have any problems with their new computers.

Unfortunately, ...

7 That's why they could print some information about the sales figures and the staff.

....

6 „Höfliche Fragen und Aussagen rund ums Essen" – Setzen Sie *some* oder *any* ein.

- *Linda*

▲ *Lucy, her mother-in-law, drops in unexpectedly*

- Oh, hello, Lucy, how nice to see you. Would you like ...some... coffee?

▲ No, thanks, I just had .... ①. But maybe I could have .... ② cake.

- I'm terribly sorry, but there isn't .... ③. What about .... ④ of our chocolate biscuits? They're freshly made.

▲ No, thanks, I prefer plain biscuits. I don't suppose you have .... ⑤, do you?

- No, I'm sorry. I don't. You really don't want anything to drink?

▲ Well, if I could have .... ⑥ tea?

- Yes, of course, I just made .... ⑦. You take milk with your tea, don't you? There is still .... ⑧ milk in the fridge. But I'm afraid I have to go shopping now before the stores close. Yesterday we had .... ⑨ people over for dinner, and there isn't .... ⑩ beer or wine left.

▲ Oh, if you go shopping, I need .... ⑪ fresh fruit. Could you get me .... ⑫ when you go to the greengrocer's?

- Of course. But I need .... ⑬ time for my shopping, because I have to go to the butcher's in town. This morning I wanted to buy .... ⑭ lamb chops in the village, but there weren't .... ⑮ in .... ⑯ of the supermarkets.

▲ Don't worry, I can wait until you come back. I'll read .... ⑰ of your fashion magazines, or maybe I'll have a little nap*.

- Okay, see you later, then.

* **to have a nap** to go to sleep

27 Die Fragewörter

1 Welche Antworten passen zu welchen Fragen?

1 Where is he from?	a I'm fine, thank you. How are you?
2 Whose computer is this?	b It begins at 10 o'clock.
3 When does the meeting start?	c I am a technician.
4 Where is the meeting?	d He is from San Francisco.
5 Who will attend the meeting?	e It is my colleague's.
6 What do you do?	f It is in the main conference room.
7 How do you do?	g All members of staff have to be present.

2 Setzen Sie die fehlenden Fragewörter ein.

1 I'm looking for my little sister. → *Who* are you looking for?

2 I'm looking for my little sister's teddy bear. → .... are you looking for?

3 She was playing with her friend. → .... was she playing with?

4 He comes from Manchester. → .... does he come from?

5 I am laughing at your jokes. → .... are you laughing at?

6 This coat is made of real Harris tweed. → .... is this coat made of?

3 Wie kann man die angegebenen Fragen noch formulieren? Setzen Sie das passende Fragepronomen ein.

1 Excuse me, could you tell me the way to the station, please? → Excuse me, *how* do I get to the station, please?

2 How much are these oranges, please? → .... much do these oranges cost?

3 How old is he? → .... is his age?

4 What time will you be back? → .... will you be back?

5 Who does this castle belong to? → .... castle is this?

6 What is the weight of your luggage? → .... heavy is your luggage?

4 *Completing a form*. Ann beantragt einen Bibliotheksausweis. Rekonstruieren Sie anhand des ausgefüllten Formulars den Dialog. Stellen Sie die passenden Fragen zu den folgenden Antworten.

Name first name	ANN	Address	
surname	THORPE	15, Oak Lane, Bath	
maiden name	PLYWOOD	Phone number	145 68 99
Date of birth	17th February 1975	~~Male~~ / Female	
Place of birth	London		
Marital Status	~~single~~ married ~~divorced~~	Children	~~yes~~ / no
Nationality	British	Occupation	Secretary
Signature	*Ann Thorpe*		

1 ● *What is your name? First name and surname, please.*
▲ My name is Ann Thorpe.

2 ● ……
▲ I was born on the 17th February 1975.

3 ● ……
▲ I was born in London.

4 ● ……
▲ I'm married.

5 ● ……
▲ I'm British.

6 ● ……
▲ I live in Bath, 15, Oak Lane. My phone number is 145 68 99.

7 ● ……
▲ I have no children.

8 ● ……
▲ I work as a secretary.

Would you like to sign here, please? Thank you very much. You'll receive your membership card in a few days.

5 Das gleiche Formular soll für eine ausländische Gaststudentin ausgefüllt werden, die einige Fragen nicht verstanden hat. Koordinieren Sie ihre Rückfragen mit den entsprechenden Auskünften der Bibliothekarin.

1 "What does maiden name mean?"	a It means job.
2 "What do you mean by nationality?"	b The word refers to the surname that you had before getting married.
3 "Could you explain the word occupation?"	c It means that you are not married.
4 "What is meant by single?"	d It means that you are a citizen of a certain country.

6 Fragen zur Zeit. Vervollständigen Sie die Lücken mit den korrekten Pronomen und antworten Sie anhand der angegebenen Informationen.

1 .... is the time, please? **5 past 10**

....

2 .... is your flight to London? **plane / to leave / 10 am**

....

3 .... does it take you to fly from Frankfurt to London? **approx. three quarters of an hour**

....

4 .... is the next train to Liverpool? **8 o'clock**

....

5 .... day is it today? **Monday**

....

6 .... is the date? **5th June, 2000**

....

7 .... does the concert start? **8 pm**

....

7 Frau Meier möchte telefonisch ein Zimmer für die Urlaubstage reservieren. Stellen Sie Fragen anhand der links angegebenen Stichwörter. Rechts sind die Antworten zu lesen.

Ms Meier: "Good morning. I would like to book a room at your hotel."

	Hotel receptionist's questions:	*Ms Meier's answers:*
1	name #	Frida Meier
2	spelling	F R I D A M E I E R
3	age	60
4	nationality	German
5	date of arrival	1st May
6	exact time of arrival	6 pm
7	length of stay	1 week
8	date of departure	7th May
9	type of accommodation required	single room

1 *What is your name, please?* ....

8 Nun stellt Frau Meier ein paar Fragen. Schließen Sie aus den Antworten der Rezeptionistin, welche es sind!

	Ms Meier's questions:	*Receptionist's answers:*
1	....	150 rooms
2	....	100 rooms with private bathrooms
3	....	TV in all the rooms
4	....	10-minute walk to the beach
5	....	breakfast between 7 and 9 am
6	....	single room £30
7	....	single room with bathroom £40
8	....	dogs are welcome

28 Das Adjektiv und das Adverb

1 Einige Worte zur Verabschiedung von Ihrer Gastgeberin. Adjektiv oder Adverb? Ergänzen Sie die korrekte Form.

1 I am terribly sorry, but I must go now.	~~terrible~~ – terribly
2 It's been a .... evening.	wonderful – wonderfully
3 The food was .... delicious.	absolute – absolutely
4 Your parties are .... the best.	simple – simply
5 I .... enjoyed myself.	real – really
6 .... I have to get up at 6 in the morning.	unfortunate – unfortunately
7 I mustn't be .... for work tomorrow.	late – lately
8 I must be off .... Thanks again. Bye.	immediate – immediately

2 „Ein kleiner Auszug aus dem Kummerkasten *(agony column)* einer Zeitschrift" – Ergänzen Sie, falls erforderlich, die Endung *-ly*.

Jane F. from Glasgow writes:

I'm twenty-four and my life is so stressful...... ①, I have literal...... ② pulled out my hair. I had to part with about half of the thick...... ③, gorgeous...... ④ mane that used to be my fantastic...... ⑤ trademark. In a few places you can actual...... ⑥ see my awful...... ⑦ scalp! My boyfriend already...... ⑧ looks at me sad...... ⑨. It is taking forever to grow back, so to speed up the process I've had a very trendy...... ⑩ haircut, used volume-enhancing...... ⑪ shampoo, and I tried extreme...... ⑫ expensive...... ⑬ hair extensions. Nothing works. Do you know any quick...... ⑭ solutions? I'm desperate...... ⑮. Please answer as soon ...... ⑯ as possible.

3 Übersetzen Sie die Antwort der Kummerkasten-Tante. Die unterstrichenen Wörter verlangen Ihre besondere Aufmerksamkeit: Adjektiv oder Adverb?

Liebe Jane,

Haare wachsen normalerweise 1 cm pro Monat. Im Sommer wachsen Sie möglicherweise ein bisschen schneller. Diesen natürlichen Prozess kann man nicht beschleunigen. Unglücklicherweise müssen Sie viel Geduld aufbringen. Um Ihre Frisur zu verdecken, tragen Sie einen schönen Schal. Oder Sie probieren es mit einem modischen Hut.

Versuchen Sie, nicht so hysterisch und nervös zu sein. Sprechen Sie mit einem guten Psychiater.

Ihre Nelly

Dear Jane, ...

....

4 Erzählen Sie Ihren Kollegen, wie Ihnen das in der abgedruckten Kritik besprochene Konzert gefallen hat. Ergänzen Sie den Lückentext, indem Sie Adjektive in Adverbien umwandeln.

Outstanding performance by the London Symphony Orchestra hits London

Last night's concert ended as a big success. The violins were extraordinary yet again. James Levine, conductor of the century, was very good indeed. The audience was enthusiastic and frenetic. They enjoyed every minute of the concert.

The London Symphony Orchestra performed *outstandingly.*

The concert ended .... ①.
The violinists played .... ②.
James Levine conducted .... ③.
The audience applauded .... ④
and .... ⑤.

5 „Ein Gespräch am Fahrkartenschalter" – Vervollständigen Sie die Sätze mit Hilfe der hier angegebenen Adjektive bzw. Adverbien.

straight far just fast ✔ near nearly hard hardly short
shortly late lately most mostly

● Excuse me, is there a fast train to London?

▲ Yes, there is. But I'm afraid you .... ① missed it.

● Oh, dear. When is the next train?

▲ Let's see. It's .... ② 8 o'clock. There is one at 9.15 that takes you .... ③ to Charing Cross Station in London.

● I'm meeting a friend outside the National Portrait Gallery at 10 o'clock.

▲ Well, that's perfect. Charing Cross is very .... ④. You won't have to walk .... ⑤.

● Will the next train be on time?

▲ I can't promise, dear. It has been punctual .... ⑥. Last month, however, the 9.15 was constantly .... ⑦. .... ⑧ passengers complained. In fact, people .... ⑨ complain about trains. They .... ⑩ appreciate how .... ⑪ we railway people are working to get things right. .... ⑫ we will introduce a spectacular high-speed train. We're all looking forward to it. There is a poster on platform one. Go and have a look.

● I'm afraid, time is too .... ⑬, it's ten past nine. You've been very kind. Thanks for the information.

6 Vervollständigen Sie die folgenden Sätze mit Hilfe des passenden Verbs aus der Auswahl. Entscheiden Sie außerdem, ob das gewählte Verb Adjektiv oder Adverb erfordert.

feel ✔ look sound taste smell

1 All the guests ...felt... *sick/~~sickly~~*. The doctor diagnosed that everybody at the party was suffering from food poisoning.

2 I might go and buy the new cookery book which was advertised on television. The recipes .... *wonderful/wonderfully*.

3 The flowers are lovely and they .... *gorgeous/gorgeously*.

4 Where did you get that dress? It .... absolutely *spectacular/ spectacularly*.

5 What is this? Hot water? This coffee .... *awful/awfully*.

7 Entscheiden Sie sich für die richtige Form.

1 Your writing is terrible. I can ...hardly... read your letter. You shouldn't go out with him. You .... ① know each other. We've got .... ② any food left. I'll have to go shopping. You've worked so .... ③. I'm sure you'll pass the exam.	hard hardly
2 The author has .... ④ been nominated for the 'Writer-of-the-Year'award; he really deserves the prize. He has .... ⑤ finished his third novel. I can't complain. He's always treated me .... ⑥. She spoke so quietly, I .... ⑦ could not hear what she said.	just justly
3 The house you're looking for is .... ⑧ the station. It is a beautiful building and .... ⑨ 200 years old. I was so exhausted, I .... ⑩ collapsed.	near nearly
4 Have you been to the theatre .... ⑪? You'll be .... ⑫ for your flight if you don't hurry up.	late lately

8 Einige Stylingtipps. Ergänzen Sie die Steigerungsformen der angegebenen Adjektive.

1 Do you want to appear taller than you are? That's easy.	tall
2 You should wear .... colours for tops.	bright
3 Buy shoes with .... heels.	high
4 Make sure you choose .... fabrics for skirts and trousers.	dark

9 „Ein Ratespiel um drei Millionärinnen" – Vervollständigen Sie die Tabelle anhand der angegebenen Informationen.

	☺ Jane	😐 Jill	☹ Julia	
income	....	$30 million	....	$130 m / $200 m
age	87 years	....	....	36 / 53 years
weight	80 kilos	....	....	79 / 98 kilos
size	....	5 ft 10	....	5 ft 4 / 6 ft 2
frame of mind	....	....	....	....

10 Ergänzen Sie nun weitere Details zu den drei Personen.

1 Jill is the youngest and Jane is the richest of the three women.

2 Julia is the heaviest of the three ladies. But she is also the tallest.

3 Jill is quite happy, but .... is happier.

4 .... is not very happy. I wonder why?

5 .... earns more money than Jill, but less than ....

6 .... is not quite as heavy as .... But they nearly weigh the same.

7 .... is shorter than ...., but not as short as ....

8 .... weighs much more than .... and ....

9 .... and .... are taller than ....

11 Vervollständigen Sie die Sätze mit dem passenden Adjektiv und entscheiden Sie sich zwischen *... than* oder *as ... as*.

entertaining expensive informative quiet safe ✔

1 Going by plane is *safer than* going by car.
2 The desert is .... Picadilly Circus.
3 Sipping champagne is .... drinking beer.
4 Playing chess is .... reading a book.
5 Listening to the news is .... reading a daily newspaper.

12 Finden Sie zu den angegebenen Adjektiven das Gegenteil! Diese acht Adjektive benötigen Sie, um die Sätze in Übung 13 zu ergänzen.

unknown	*popular*	sad	*f _ _ _ _*
interesting	*b _ _ _ _ _*	ugly	*p _ _ _ _ _*
boring	*e _ _ _ _ _ _ _*	ordinary	*s _ _ _ _ _ _ _*
aggressive	*g e _ _ _ _*	bad	*g _ _ _*

13 Ergänzen Sie die Sätze mit dem Superlativ der vorigen Adjektive.

1 The Rolling Stones are one of the *most popular* rock bands.
3 Many people agree that cricket is one of the .... sports.
4 Football, however, is generally accepted to be one of the .... games.
5 A Labrador is known to be one of the .... dogs.
6 Charlie Chaplin will always be remembered as one of the .... actors.
7 Kate Moss is one of the .... models.
8 Michael Jordan is definitely one of the .... basketball players.
9 Champagne is one of the .... beverages.

14 Kombinieren Sie die beiden passenden Satzhälften!

The ...

1 The more I got to know him,
2 The thicker the coat,
3 The more you have,
4 The older the wine,
5 The longer she had to wait,
6 The more you buy,
7 The more you try,

the bigger the taste.
the more nervous she became.
the more you want.
the more likely you are to succeed.
the heavier our shopping bag.
the more I appreciated his good manners.
the warmer it'll keep you in winter.

... the ...

15 "As ... as" – Vervollständigen Sie die folgenden feststehenden bildhaften Vergleiche.

1 as fast as ....
2 as easy as ....
3 as heavy as ....
4 as thin as a ....
5 as good as ....
6 as stubborn as a ....
7 as strong as an ....
8 as pretty as a ....

a ox
b ABC
c rake
d gold
e mule
f lightening
g lead
h picture

16 „Ein unvergessliches Rendezvous" – Verbinden Sie die zwei Sätze mit *Not only*. Achten Sie auf die Inversion!

1 He had me waiting for half an hour. He didn't even bother apologizing to me when he finally arrived.

2 He was very rude to the waiter. He upset all other guests by being so noisy and telling them to shut up.

3 His main topic of conversation was, of course, himself. He accused me of not being able to listen to other people's problems.

4 He was eating noisily. He was talking with his mouth full.

5 He forgot his credit card. He had no cash with him.

6 I had to pay for the meal. He asked me if I could lend him some money.

7 He was drunk. He asked me if I could get him a taxi and pay for it.

8 This was the most embarrassing date I've ever had. It was also one of the costliest.

1 *Not only did he have me waiting for half an hour, he didn't even bother apologizing when he finally arrived.*

2 ....

3 ....

4 ....

5 ....

6 ....

7 ....

8 ....

29 Die Präpositionen

1 Geographische Standorte. Setzen Sie die Präpositionen ein.

on ✔ on on off in in in to

1 New York is ..on.... the east coast of the United States.
2 St. Louis is .... the river Mississippi.
3 Long Island is .... the coast of the United States.
4 Boulder is a city .... the Rocky Mountains.
5 Texas is .... the south of the United States.
6 Chicago is .... Lake Michigan.
7 Mount McKinley is .... Alaska.
8 Washington D.C. is .... the south of Philadelphia.

2 *in, at* oder *on* – alle können räumliche Zuordnungen beschreiben. Vervollständigen Sie die folgende Beschreibung.

I live .... ① New York City. My apartment is .... ② Euston Street .... ③ Lower Manhattan. It is .... ④ the 5th floor, but there is a lift .... ⑤ the building. I work .... ⑥ an investment bank .... ⑦ Wall Street. When I'm .... ⑧ my office, I spend all day sitting .... ⑨ my desk. Sometimes I get up and put something .... ⑩ the shelf or .... ⑪ the cupboard, but not very often. .... ⑫ my way to work I buy a sandwich .... ⑬ the baker's. I take the entrance .... ⑭ the back of the company building. It's quicker than .... ⑮ the front entrance. .... ⑯ home I love sitting .... ⑰ my armchair reading the sports section .... ⑱ the newspaper. In summer I like sunbathing .... ⑲ Central Park and watching the hustle and bustle around me.

3 „Linda hinterlässt eine Nachricht auf dem Anrufbeantworter von Pete" – Vervollständigen Sie die Lücken.

British Airways No. 705 MUC 11.45 am MAN 1.20 pm

1 Hi, Pete, this is Linda. I've just booked our flight to Manchester.
Flight No. 705 leaves Munich at 11.45 .... the morning.

2 Try and be at the airport .... time. Don't turn up .... the last minute. I don't want us to miss the flight.

3 The plane arrives in Manchester .... 1.20 .... the afternoon.

4 If there are any questions, call me this evening. I'll be at home .... 10 o'clock. See you tomorrow.

4 Weitere Präpositionen der Zeit. Füllen Sie die Lücken aus.

1 I'll see you early .... the evening.

2 Let me finish this chapter first. I'll be with you .... five minutes.

3 I'll talk to you .... two or three weeks then.

4 Let's meet .... Friday.

5 Shall we go and see the manager some time .... the afternoon?

6 I'm going away .... the end of January.

7 Most people work .... nine .... five.

8 The museum closes .... noon.

9 The official start of the theatre season is .... August.

10 The restaurant closes .... 11 o'clock .... night.

11 My brother's birthday is .... July. He was born .... 1970.

12 The meeting is .... the 5th September .... ten past eight .... the morning.

5 ***How do I get to ....?*** **Eine Wegbeschreibung. Suchen Sie aus der Liste die passenden Möglichkeiten heraus.**

Turn right.
Take the second turning to the left.
Go down this road. ✔
You'll see the bank on your left.
When you get to the church, turn left.
Go straight down this road.
Turn right at the crossing.
Keep straight on.

1 Gehen Sie diese Straße entlang.
Go down this road.
....
....

2 Biegen Sie rechts ab.
....

3 Biegen Sie bei der Kirche links ab.
....

4 An der Kreuzung biegen Sie rechts ab.
....

5 Biegen Sie die zweite Straße nach links ab.
....

6 Die Bank ist auf der linken Straßenseite.
....

30 Die Zahlen

1 Michael ist ein begeisterter Kinogänger und sieht sich die Filme immer in der englischen Originalversion an. Alle seine Lieblingsfilme haben eine Ordnungszahl im Titel. Wie heißen sie?

1 *„Der Club der Teufelinnen"*
"The First Wives Club"

„Der erste Ritter"
"The .... Knight"

2 *„Der zweite Mann"*
....

3 *„Unheimliche Begegnung der Dritten Art"*
"Close Encounters of the .... Kind"

„Der dritte Mann"
....

4 *„Geboren am Vierten Juli"*
"Born on the .... of July"

5 *„Das fünfte Element"*
....

6 *„Der sechste Sinn"*
"The .... Sense"

7 *„Das siebte Kreuz"*
....

8 *„Blaubarts achte Frau"*
....

9 *„Die neun Pforten"*
"The .... Gate"

10 *„Der dreizehnte Krieger"*
"The .... Warrior"

2 Wie werden die Rechenarten im Englischen formuliert?

add up to ✔ to be divisable by to divide by to equal to multiply by to multiply by plus minus

1 15 and 17 add up to 32.
2 5 .... 5 equals 25.
3 40 .... 8.
4 28 .... 4 .... 7.
5 63 .... 13 equals 50.
6 8 .... 9 equals 72.
7 52 .... 7 equals 45.
8 52 .... 7 equals 59.

3 „Vom Versuch, einen Termin zu vereinbaren" – Peter und Paul unterhalten sich. Übersetzen Sie das Gespräch, in dem natürlich sehr viele Zahlen auftauchen.

● *Peter* ▲ *Paul*

● Wie wäre es am 14. Februar um 13 Uhr?

▲ Das geht leider nicht. Meine Maschine landet erst um 12 Uhr Mittag, und die Fahrt vom Flughafen in die Stadt dauert ungefähr eine Stunde und vierzig Minuten. Doch wir könnten uns am späten Nachmittag im Café treffen?

● Am Nachmittag um Viertel nach Fünf habe ich leider eine Besprechung.

▲ Lässt sich das nicht verschieben?

● Leider nein. Es ist eine Besprechung mit einem unserer wichtigsten Kunden. Er bezieht Waren im Wert von 1,57 Milliarden Dollar. Das entspricht zwei Drittel unseres gesamten Jahresumsatzes.

▲ Wir könnten uns am 1. Mai zu einem Tennisspiel treffen.

● Das geht nicht. Mein Chef hat Geburtstag. Er wird achtzig. Gleichzeitig wird das dreißigjährige Bestehen der Firma gefeiert.

▲ In vierzehn Tagen hätte ich vielleicht Zeit. Wie wäre es mit einem Abendessen? Am Mittwoch, den 3. Februar?

● Das passt gut. Es gibt ein neues Restaurant in der Neal Street Nr. 15. Es ist in 10 Minuten von hier zu Fuß zu erreichen. Du gehst bis zur Kreuzung, dann die vierte Querstraße links. Es ist ein altes Haus aus dem Jahr 1899. Das Café ist im 3. Stock. Es heißt TIME OUT.

4 In der folgenden Übung dreht sich erneut alles um Zahlen. Ergänzen Sie die Sätze mit den entsprechenden Formulierungen aus dem Pool. Sicher können Sie erraten, welche die jeweils passende ist!

seventh heaven first come, first served number one ✔ two and two
two-faced sixes and sevens seven-year-itch one in a million
six of one and half a dozen of the other sixth sense first

1 Your friend puts himself first before everyone else. He is completely selfish.
He takes care of *number one*.

2 Ever since they fell in love they've been in .... They're extremely happy.

3 I can put .... together. There is enough evidence that you've eaten all the crisps, for instance, the empty bags are still in your garbage bin.

4 You are .... You are such a valuable and unusual person. You're very special, indeed.

5 He is such a .... person. He's insincere and quite an opportunist. He criticizes his colleagues behind their backs. When they're around, however, he's awfully nice to them.

6 In 1914 some people who had booked the Atlantic voyage on the Titanic decided not to embark on the ship. They must have had .... They somehow knew the ship was never to return from its maiden voyage.

7 I'm totally confused and can't make up my mind. I'm at .... this week.

8 I'm sorry I can't go to the cinema today. I have to study for my exam next week. My exam comes ....

9 ● Shall we go to your place or mine?

▲ I don't know, it's .... It really makes no difference to me.

10 My brother has the .... He is feeling dissatisfied with his marriage. After seven years, he is thinking of starting a relationship with another woman.

11 What a shame! I arrived only five minutes later than I had planned, and all the tickets for the concert had been distributed. They would have been free tickets and were given away on a .... basis.

5 Ordnen Sie die Erklärungen den passenden Formulierungen zu.

A

1 first aid	a of the highest quality
2 first-class	b ~ information is information gained directly from its source
3 first-hand	c medical treatment given to an injured person

B

1 two-piece	a if something, e.g. a remark, can be interpreted in two ways
2 two-faced	b a ~ suit: a jacket and trousers, but no waistcoat
3 two-edged	c insincere and hypocritical

C

1 three-dimensional	a reading, (w)riting, (a)rithmetic
2 three quarters	b having length, breadth and depth
3 the three R's	c three parts out of four

D

1 four-wheel	a a group of four people
2 on all fours	b the car has a ~ drive: all wheels are connected to the source of power
3 foursome	c on hands and knees

E

1 sixth form	a the number of students increased ~, in other words, we now have six times as many students as last year
2 sixfold	b package containing six units, e.g. six cans of beer
3 sixpack	c the most senior class in a secondary school for pupils over sixteen

Lösungen

1 Die Gegenwart: einfache Form und *ing*-Form

1

Endung -es: rushes, fetches, mixes, relaxes
Endung -ies: relies, carries, marries, copies
Endung -s: shows, buys, lies, says, grows

2

1 – b; 2 – a; 3 – a; 4 – d; 5 – b; 6 – a; 7 – b; 8 – d; 9 – c

3

1 – c; 2 –b; 3 – d; 4 – b; 5 – a; 6 – e; 7 – b; 8 – b; 9 – e

4

1 is playing; 2 is playing; 3 play; 4 is raining; 5 rains; 6 is staying; 7 stays; 8 isn't working; 9 doesn't work; 10 am writing; 11 write; 12 is baking (*oder:* bakes); 13 bake; 14 bakes; 15 bakes

5

1 are always leaving (*oder:* always leave); 2 is always complaining (*oder:* always complain), is now playing, usually plays; 3 is always going away (*oder:* always goes away), regularly goes away; 4 are always having, always serves

6

1 is; 2 practises; 3 doesn't (*oder:* does not) play; 4 is; 5 is making; 6 doesn't (*oder:* does not) matter; 7 are; 8 is shining; 9 is; 10 goes; 11 digs; 12 is getting; 13 is snoring; 14 snores; 15 am warning (*oder:* warn); 16 is; 17 talks; 18 is; 19 is walking; 20 are; 21 are dancing; 22 call; 23 love; 24 are; 25 are joking; 26 are not telling; 27 tell; 28 is knocking; 29 wonder

2 Die Vergangenheit *(Past Tense)*: einfache Form und *ing*-Form

1

Endung -ed: walked, played, suffered, pulled, listened, watched,
Endung Verdoppelung und -ed: travelled, plugged, labelled, preferred, benefitted
-y > -ied: married, tried, hurried, replied

2

1 married, lived, encountered; 2 preferred; 3 suffered, moved, disappeared; 4 scrubbed; 5 poured, unplugged; 6 used

3

1 walked; 2 met, married; 3 lost; 4 collected; 5 panicked; 6 tipped; 7 tried, missed

4

I halved a melon and removed the seeds. Then I made melon balls with a scoop and chilled them. I peeled a grapefruit with a sharp knife. I cut the fruit into segments. I sprinkled the grapefruit segments with sugar. I allowed them to stand at room temperature for 30 minutes. I grated enough rind from two lemons to give 2 tablespoons. I squeezed the juice of 2 lemons. I added the grapefruit and melon balls, then puréed everything in a blender. I added enough water to give half a litre of liquid. I stirred well. I tasted and added sugar. I served the cocktail in frosted glasses. I sprinkled the glasses with lemon grind. I garnished the cocktail with green mint leaves and a slice of lemon.

5

1 While I was clearing the breakfast table my husband left for work. 2 While I was doing the ironing I was watching television. 3 While I was taking the dog out for a walk I was thinking about a nice birthday present for my mother-in-law. 4 I remembered that I had to pick up clothes at the dry cleaner's while I was putting the dirty clothes into the washing machine. 5 While I was making the beds I was listening to the radio. 6 While I was working in the garden the postman rang the doorbell. 7 While I was cleaning the windows it started raining. 8 While I was hoovering the flat I realized it was time to think about dinner. 9 While I was looking through my cookery book I discovered a nice recipe for fish and chips. 10 While I was peeling the potatoes and cutting them into sections my mother dropped in for a cup of tea. 11 While I was laying the table my husband came home from work. 12 While I was opening a bottle of wine he was sitting at the table and looked forward to his dinner.

7

1 didn't call; 2 fell asleep; 3 was; 4 wore; 5 wore; 6 prepared; 7 cleaned; 8 left; 9 had; 10 drove; 11 took; 12 had; 13 felt; 14 woke me up; 15 returned; 16 went; 17 talked; 18 spent; 19 looked

8

say, says, saying, said
choose, chooses, choosing, chose
try, tries, trying, tried
do, does, doing, did
have, has, having, had
eat, eats, eating, ate
hope, hopes, hoping, hoped
supply, supplies, supplying, supplied
begin, begins, beginning, began
develop, develops, developing, developed
agree, agrees, agreeing, agreed
argue, argues, arguing, argued

3 Die einfache Vergangenheit *(Past Tense)* und das *Present Perfect*

1

1 bought; 2 paid; 3 spent; 4 heard; 5 read; 6 had; 7 made; 8 fed; 9 travelled

2

1 been; 2 chosen; 3 robbed; 4 hidden; 5 eaten; 6 drunk; 7 seen

3

1 because I have been watching television all night. 2 because I have been spending too much time sitting at the computer. 3 because I have been eating too many garlic and onion canapes. 4 because I haven't been getting enough sleep. 5 because I have been doing too many stretching exercises. 6 because I have been eating too many chocolates. 7 because I have been smoking too many cigarettes. 8 because I have been drinking too much. 9 because I have been walking around in high heels all day. 10 because I have been sunbathing all day. 11 because I have been walking in the rain. 12 because I have been carrying heavy shopping bags.

4

1 have lived; 2 lived; 3 moved; 4 have been able to; 5 have attended; 6 hasn't smoked; 7 saw; 8 has seen; 9 went; 10 have been; 11 have been; 12 hasn't turned up

5

1 had, has recovered; 2 stayed, have made; 3 have lost, haven't found; 4 haven't seen; 5 haven't you (*oder:* have you not) come; 6 have … finished; 7 Have … been, visited

6

1 have lived; 2 have lived; 3 is; 4 was; 5 is; 6 isn't working; 7 have you been; 8 have been; 9 began; 10 have you changed; 11 have had; 12 left

7

1 have been asking; 2 have been arguing; 3 haven't been listening; 4 have been trying; 5 have been neglecting

4 Das *Past Perfect*

1

1 had been trying; 2 had been searching, had been wearing; 3 had been raining, had forgotten; 4 had arranged, was waiting, wasn't turning up; 5 was shopping, had forgotten; 6 was enjoying, have forgotten, hadn't forgotten; 7 was walking, had parked

2

1 By the time the other guests arrived he had eaten most of the party sandwiches. 2 He was sick because he had eaten too much. 3 His girlfriend was very angry and decided to ignore him all evening because he had forgotten to dance with her. 4 A horrible stain appeared on the white table cloth when he had spilt some red wine. 5 He couldn't go home by car and had to walk home because he had drunk too much at the party. 6 Nobody wanted to drive him home because he had annoyed so many people at the party. 7 He got soaking wet because he had forgotten to put on his coat and it was raining. 8 By the time he remembered that he carried a raincoat in his rucksack he had caught a cold. 9 He had walked ten miles in the pouring rain before a car stopped and offered him a ride. 10 By the time he arrived home the rain had stopped. 11 He couldn't open the door to his flat because he had lost his keys. 12 All of a sudden he remembered the spare key under the doormat when he had rung his neighbour's door bell. 13 He only suffered from a slight hangover the next morning because his friendly neighbour had made him a pot of coffee.

5 Die Zukunftsformen

1

1 are going to, will; 2 are going to, will; 3 will; 4 are going to; 5 is going to; 6 will; 7 will (*oder:* is going to); 8 is going to, will (*oder:* is going to); 9 will, will; 10 is going to (*oder:* will), is going to (*oder:* will), will (*oder:* is going to), will (*oder:* is going to)

2

1 are having; 2 are having; 3 are playing; 4 are attending; 5 are giving; 6 are meeting; 7 are appearing; 8 are leaving; 9 are giving; 10 are arriving

3

1 are taking, closes, takes; 2 are going, starts; 3 are visiting, arrives; 4 is starting, starts, ends; 5 am … staying, leaves; 6 are having, is; 7 am going, have; 8 are buying, cost, are

4

1 Will you go out; 2 will be going; 3 will get on (*oder:* will be getting on); 4 will you recognise; 5 will have (*oder:* will be having); 6 will he know; 7 will be wearing; 8 will he pick; 9 will be meeting; 10 will you be doing; 11 will be having; 12 will go; 13 will enjoy; 14 will be; 15 will have (*oder:* be having)

5

1 Will you open the window, please? 2 Will you close the window, please? 3 Will you get us some tea or coffee, please? 4 Will you speak up, please? 5 Will you ring for a taxi, please? 6 Will you excuse me, please? 7 Will you pass on a message, please? 8 Will you remind me to phone the baker's, please? 9 Will you sign the letter, please? 10 Will you send off the invitations, please?

6

1 will have had; 2 will have worked; 3 will have reached; 4 will have been; 5 will have started; 6 will have faded away; 7 will have gone; 8 will have tried; 9 will have gone; 10 will have decided; 11 will have become

6 Das Passiv

1

1 is served; 2 are boiled; 3 are prepared; 4 are fried; 5 is served; 6 is served

2

1 Our perfume is sold in <u>flasks</u>. 2 Whisky is stored in <u>barrels</u>. 3 Whisky is bought in <u>bottles</u>. 4 Milk is filled in <u>cartons or bottles</u>. 5 Marmalade can be bought in <u>jars</u>. 6 Crisps are packed in <u>bags</u>. 7 Bottled beer is delivered in <u>crates</u>. 8 Our catfood is delivered in <u>tins</u>. 9 Chewing gum is sold in <u>packets</u>. 10 Ice-cream is offered in <u>tubs</u>. 11 Margarine is bought in a <u>tub</u>.

3

1 they; 2 it; 3 they; 4 it; 5 it; 6 they; 7 it; 8 it; 9 it; 10 they; 11 it

4

1 They are jotted down by the writer. 2 It is written by him. 3 They are fleshed out by him. 4 It is finished by him. 5 It is sent to the editor of his local newspaper. 6 They are printed in the weekend edition by the editor. 7 It is offered to a publisher by the author. 8 If he likes it, it will be published as a hardcover book. 9 Later, it is offered by the bookshops. 10 They are sold by the shops in the first year. 11 It is translated into many languages by leading literary translators.

5

1 It is believed that the novel will be reviewed by critics. 2 It is known that the property will be bought by a Hollywood film producer. 3 It is reported that the author will be asked by the producer to turn the novel into a film script. 4 It is understood that the film based on the novel will be released by a distributor. 5 It is alleged that the film will be loved by cinemagoers all over the world. 6 It is said that the Nobel prize for literature will be awarded to the author by the jury. 7 It is understood that the Oscar in the category Best Film Production of the Year will be won by the Hollywood film producer.

6

1 The opera 'Porgy and Bess' was composed by George Gershwin. 2 Many famous churches and other buildings in London were designed by Sir Christopher Wren. 3 England was conquered by William the Conquerer. 4 The miniskirt was created by Mary Quant. 5 The part of Scarlet O'Hara in 'Gone with the Wind' was played by Vivian Leigh. 6 The films 'Lawrence of Arabia' and 'Doctor Zhivago' were directed by David Lean. 7 The play 'King Lear' was written by Shakespeare. 8 Australia and New Zealand were discovered by James Cook. 9 The steam engine was invented by James Watt. 10 The phrase 'Ich bin ein Berliner' was coined by John F. Kennedy.

7

1 He is said to have been a spy for the KGB. 2 to have had a nervous breakdown. 3 to regularly use the personal services of Madame Fifi. 4 to have left him. 5 to live with a male model twenty years younger than herself. 6 to have been facelifted ten times over the past two years. 7 to spend a fortune on clothes. 8 is thought to allow her to marry him because she is rolling in money. 9 is known to have had an affair with Lord Sinclair's younger daughter and to have dropped her when the other woman came along. 10 is reported to have given a live interview on television talking about all the details of their love life. 11 is said to be not capable of keeping anything to herself.

7 Die *ing*-Form als Gerundium und der Infinitiv

1

1 Missing; 2 Being; 3 Falling; 4 Making; 5 Keeping; 6 Having; 7 Educating; 8 Dancing; 9 Drowning; 10 Looking; 11 Killing; 12 Knocking (*oder:* Knockin')

2

1 going to the cinema regularly. 2 reading the Financial Times every day. 3 on supporting the World Wildlife Fund and similar organisations. 4 going to Old Trafford to see my favourite team playing. 5 of moving to the United States. 6 trying tap dancing myself. 7 of reading novels and short stories. 8 in knowing more about other painting techniques. 9 on learning languages. 10 to organising my next trip around the world. 11 doing nothing or lying in bed and watching old Hollywood movies on television. 12 hanging around in cafés and meeting friends.

3

1 to spend; 2 to improve, to improve; 3 to be getting; 4 to develop; 5 to be; 6 to adopt; 7 to come up; 8 getting; 9 reducing; 10 dismissing, to go, to be able

4

1 used to believe, thinks, having; 2 used to be, is; 3 used to live, is; 4 used to eat, is; 5 used to love, suits; 6 used to hate, drives; 7 used to prefer, enjoys; 8 used to call, is, thinks

8 Das Partizip

1

1 Having been woken up by the sound of the alarm clock I get up. 2 Having taken a shower I get dressed. 3 Having breakfast I watch breakfast TV. 4 Driving to work I listen to the news on the radio. 5 Having worked from 9 to 5 I go home. 6 Having eaten something I go to the local pub. 7 Drinking 2 pints of beer I talk to colleagues and friends. 8 Having come home I set the alarm clock. 9 Thinking about what happened during the day I fall asleep.

2

1 Being such a narcissist; 2 Being such a scaremonger; 3 Being such a coward; 4 Being such a bore; 5 Being such a pessimist; 6 Being such a gossip; 7 Being such a fusspot; 8 Being such a yes-man

3

1 come, leaving; 2 crawling; 3 touch; 4 howling; 5 lock; 6 climbing; 7 whisper; 8 burning; 9 swearing

9 Die *if*-Sätze

1

1 if; 2 when, If; 3 If, When, if; 4 If; 5 If; 6 When, if; 7 if, when; 8 if, If, When, when

2

1 If I didn't have to work, I would come to your party. 2 If it wasn't looking like it's going to rain any minute, we could go for a walk. 3 If I didn't have this terrible headache, I could go out with you. 4 If I weren't always so busy, I would visit you more often. 5 If I hadn't arranged to meet my parents, I could have lunch with you today. 6 If you weren't always talking with your mouth full, I would have dinner with you. 7 If I didn't have visitors this weekend, I could babysit for you. 8 If my place wasn't in a complete mess, I would ask you to come upstairs for a drink. 9 If I hadn't promised my girlfriend to go shopping with her, I could help you with your packing. 10 If we were more alike and had more in common, I would marry you.

3

Yes:

1 If you like the combination of teamsports, bodychecks and ice-skating, ice-hockey is the type of sport I would recommend. 2 If you admire people like Boris Becker and Andre Agassi, tennis seems to be your kind of sport. 3 If altitude sickness is a problem for you, you shouldn't try paragliding or parachuting or hang gliding. 4 If you are very tall, playing basketball or doing the highjump would be a good idea. 5 If you like horses, you should go in for horse racing or other equestrian sports. 6 If you have good stamina and like long-distance running, I recommend marathon running. 7 If you like fast cars and are obsessed with speed, motor racing is your cup of tea. 8 If you prefer team sports and games that go on for hours if not for days, I recommend cricket. 9 If you like rough sports, you should join a rugby club or play American football.

No:

1 If you don't like the combination of teamsports, bodychecks and ice-skating, ice-hockey isn't the type of sport I would recommend. 2 If you don't admire people like Boris Becker and Andre Agassi, tennis doesn't seem to be your kind of sport. 3 If altitude sickness isn't a (*oder:* is no) problem for you, you

should try paragliding or parachuting, or even hang-gliding maybe. 4 If you aren't very tall, playing basketball or doing the highjump wouldn't be a good idea. 5 If you don't like horses, you shouldn't go in for horse racing or other equestrian sports. 6 If you don't have good stamina and like long-distance running, I don't recommend marathon running. 7 If you don't like fast cars and aren't obsessed with speed, motor racing isn't your cup of tea. 8 If you don't prefer team sports and games that go on for hours if not for days, I don't recommend cricket. 9 If you don't like rough sports, you shouldn't join a rugby club or play American football.

4

1 If I hadn't watched, would have had; 2 If they hadn't shown, wouldn't have spent; 3 If I had had, would have studied; 4 If I had worked, would have covered; 5 If I had learned (*oder:* learnt), would have been; 6 If I hadn't had, would have slept; 7 If I had been able, wouldn't have made; 8 If I hadn't followed, wouldn't have failed; 9 If I hadn't watched, wouldn't have written

10 Die unvollständigen Hilfsverben

1

1 Joe is said to drink three bottles of whisky every day. 2 He is said to eat ten hard-boiled eggs for breakfast. 3 He is said to sleep on a bed of nails. 4 Such torture is meant to gradually kill off all feelings of pain. 5 He is supposed to have robbed fifty banks when he was younger. 6 The bank robberies were meant to show the whole world that rules and regulations were not for him and that he is in a class of his own. 7 He is said to have 30 children. 8 This was meant to prove that he was a real womanizer. 9 He is said to have killed a lion with his bare hands. 10 Joe's father Jim is said to have been a hunter in Africa and a famous bullfighter in Spain. 11 Jim was to be an ardent admirer of Ernest Hemingway. 12 And later, Jim was to be the hero of many little boys – including his own son. 13 A film producer is supposed to do a documentary about Joe's many adventures. 14 Joe is said to publish some of his poems next year. This is intended to show that he's got brains not just brawn. 15 Joe intends to write his memoirs. 16 He is supposed to do a promotional tour to sell the book. 17 This was supposed to be the start of his second career as a writer.

2

1 – F; 2 – E; 3 – E; 4 – E; 5 – F; 6 – E; 7 – F

3

1 Would you ask your mother whether you may lend me some money? 2 May my brother borrow your car? 3 May I use your pocket calculator? 4 I may play the piano between 3 and 6 o'clock in the afternoon.

4

1 mustn't, must, is not allowed, are not allowed; 2 can, are not allowed; 3 must, mustn't; 4 are not allowed, must, is not allowed; 5 are allowed, mustn't, must; 6 mustn't; 7 can; 8 mustn't, is not allowed

5

1 I should have worked harder. 2 I should have attended classes more regularly. 3 I shouldn't have missed so many lessons. 4 I should have done my homework every day. 5 I should have gone out less. 6 I should have listened to my professor's lectures more carefully. 7 I shouldn't have overslept so often. 8 I shouldn't have always been late for classes. 9 I should have spent the weekends studying rather than partying. 10 I should have tried to avoid last year's mistakes. 11 I should have convinced myself that school isn't so bad after all.

6

1 mustn't, must (*oder:* have to); 2 mustn't, needn't; 3 mustn't; 4 mustn't; 5 mustn't, needn't

11 Die indirekte Rede

1

Patricia told me that

1 she had wonderful news. 2 <u>the day before</u> (*oder:* <u>the previous day</u>) she had had a pregnancy test done. 3 she was three months pregnant. 4 the baby will be due in March next year. 5 she should have known herself because every morning she had woken up feeling ill. 6 she had felt sick in the mornings during the first couple of days of her pregnancy. 7 she had given up smoking when she found out. 8 she had been reading many books about how to be a good mother. 9 they were going away for a few days because she needed a rest. 10 eventually she was going to give up work. 11 I could come and babysit for her if I liked.

2

Jill said that

1 John had asked her to marry him <u>two months before</u>. 2 she had been in love with him for many years. 3 she had said yes. 4 they were getting married on 5th June. 5 that (day) would be the happiest day of her life. 7 they would spend their honeymoon on the Bahamas.

She asked me if

6 I would be able to come to their wedding.

3

<u>Horizontal</u>: state, admit, reply, explain, add, answer

<u>Vertikal</u>: say, tell, explain, remark

5

1 what her (*oder:* their) holiday had been (*oder:* was) like, it had been (*oder:* was) marvellous and that they had had (*oder:* had) a great time.

2 where she (*oder:* they) had gone (*oder:* went), they had gone (*oder:* went) to the Greek island of Rhodes. 3 who she had gone (*oder:* went) with, she had gone (*oder:* went) with her husband. 4 where exactly they had stayed (*oder:* stayed), they had stayed (*oder:* stayed) at a small hotel. 5 what the weather had been (*oder:* was) like, the weather (*oder:* it) had been (*oder:* was) great and that they had had (*oder:* had) sunshine every day. 6 how they had spent (*oder:* spent) their time, they had gone (*oder:* went) for walks in the evening and had done (*oder:* did) a lot of sunbathing.

6

1 whether (*oder:* if) we are free next Saturday. 2 whether (*oder:* if) 7 pm is too early. 3 whether (*oder:* if) we would like to have dinner at their place. 4 whether (*oder:* if) we are interested in last year's photographs, too. 5 whether (*oder:* if) we'll come by car or whether (*oder:* if) we'll take the underground. 6 whether (*oder:* if) we want her to draw a map to show us how to get to their house.
7 whether (*oder:* if) we'll bring our (*oder:* the) kids.

7

1 they were not only serving drinks, but also food? (*oder:* they were serving drinks and food? *oder:* they were serving also food?) 2 it wasn't a fancy dress party and that nobody was wearing fancy clothes. 3 there would be live music.
4 nobody was giving (any) presents to the hosts.

8

1 that we might have to wait five or ten minutes at the entrance. 2 to queue at the end of the line. 3 not to jump the queue. 4 not to take bags or umbrellas into the museum. 5 that we needn't (*oder:* didn't need to, didn't have to) worry about our belongings – their cloakroom was never unattended. 6 not to leave (*oder:* that we weren't allowed to leave) the marked path. 7 that we could take photographs provided we didn't use a flash. 8 that we had to follow the directions of their personnel.

12 Der Imperativ

1

1 Study more. 2 Work harder. 3 Don't miss so many lessons. 4 Do your homework every day. 5 Go out less. 6 Sleep in less often. 7 Don't be late for classes. 8 Try to avoid last year's mistakes.

2

1 Spend; 2 Stay; 3 Don't chat; 4 Don't spend; 5 Get out; 6 Change

13 Die *Phrasal Verbs*

1

1 – d; 2 – c; 3 – e; 4 – a; 5 – b

2

1 look for; 2 looking after; 3 look up; 4 looking forward; 5 looking for; 6 looked up; 7 look after

3

<u>turn on/off</u>: light, television, water, heating, cooker
<u>switch on/off</u>: light, television, cooker
<u>put on/off</u>: light, television
<u>turn up/down</u>: heating, volume

4

1 I'm afraid I can't <u>put up with</u> this noise any more. 2 Our friends offered to <u>put you up</u>. 3 We'<u>ve been putting off</u> the decision whether to buy a new car or book a trip around the world. 4 Why don't you <u>put on</u> your new dress? 5 Pick up all your toys and <u>put them away</u> in the toy box.

5
1 get on with; 2 getting out of; 3 get off; 4 get up; 5 get away; 6 Get on

14 Der Konjunktiv

1
1 – c; 2 – d; 3 – e; 4 – b; 5 – a

2
1 God bless them; 2 come what may; 3 be that as it may; 4 be it right or wrong; 5 If need be

15 Frageform und Verneinung

1
1 Who are you looking for? 2 What are you looking for? 3 Who was she playing with? 4 Where does he come from? 5 Which part of town does he live in? 6 What are you laughing at? 7 What is this coat made of? 8 What were you talking about?

2
1 is not / isn't; 2 has not / hasn't; 3 does not do / doesn't do; 4 cannot / can't; 5 does not learn / doesn't learn; 6 does not seem / doesn't seem; 7 does not speak / doesn't speak; 8 is not / isn't; 9 will not / won't

3
1 Do you think it's going to snow? 2 Was it raining last night? 3 Did it snow three years ago on 1st November? (*oder:* Didn't it snow three years ago on 1st November?) 4 Did the weather turn dull a few days ago? (*oder:* When did the weather turn dull?) 5 Do you think it's going to stop raining? (*oder:* Is it going to stop raining?, Isn't it going to stop raining?)

4
1 is it; 2 does she; 3 are you; 4 didn't we; 5 isn't there; 6 wouldn't you; 7 would you; 8 don't you; 9 shall we

16 Der unbestimmte Artikel

1
1 a, a; 2 an, a; 3 a, a, a; 4 a, a; 5 a, an; 6 a, an; 7 an, a

2
1 a, /; 2 a; 3 /; 4 /; 5 /; 6 /; 7 an, /; 8 a

3
What a beautiful morning! What terrible weather! What rotten luck!
What a fantastic view! What a fool I've been! What a good idea!
What beautiful scenery! What a genius he is! What luck! What a man!

4
1 What luck! 2 What rotten luck! 3 What <u>a</u> beautiful morning! 4 What <u>a</u> fantastic view! 5 What terrible weather! 6 What <u>a</u> fool I've been! 7 What <u>a</u> genius he is! 8 what <u>a</u> man! 9 What beautiful scenery! 10 What <u>a</u> good idea!

17 Der bestimmte Artikel

1
1 – b; 2 – e; 3 – g; 4 – a; 5 – d; 6 – i; 7 – c; 8 – f

2
1 church; 2 the hospital; 3 the hospital; 4 school, work; 5 hospital; 6 the church; 7 prison; 8 bed; 9 university; 10 the school

3
<u>Horizontal</u>: drums, violin, trumpet, composer, clarinet
<u>Vertikal</u>: piano, guitar, bandleader, saxophone

4
1 the guitar; 2 guitar, guitar; 3 the trumpet; 4 the piano; 5 the clarinet; 6 the saxophone; 7 the violin; 8 the drums; 9 the, bandleaders; 10 The composer, the

5
1 the, an, the; 2 the, the, the, the, /; 3 the; 4 the, the, the, a; 5 the, a, the, the, /, a; 6 the, the

6
1 /; 2 the, the; 3 the; 4 /; 5 /, the; 6 the; 7 the, /

18 Das Substantiv – die Pluralbildung

1

1 strength; 2 patience; 3 advantage; 4 mystery; 5 pride; 6 sarcasm; 7 true; 8 generous; 9 energetic; 10 ambitious; 11 long
Lösungswort: sentimental
Substantiv: sentiment

2

-s: computers, cars, bicycles, reports, disks, desks, telephones, papers, toys, meetings, colleagues, breaks, offices, chairs, cupboards, pencils, plays
-es: bosses, buses, faxes, passes
y > ies: companies, hobbies, mysteries

3

1 newspapers; 2 kilos; 3 wives; 4 loaves, halves; 5 hobbies; 6 scarfs (*oder:* scarves); 7 photos; 8 potatoes; 9 mangos (*oder:* mangoes), avocados (*oder:* avocadoes)

19 Das Substantiv – der Genitiv

1

Personen: 1, 7; Tiere: 2, 8; Orte, Länder: 9; Zeitangaben: 4, 5; Dinge: 3, 10; Abstrakta: 6

2

1 the Queen's visit to Berlin; 2 the protection of the environment; 3 this year's crop; 4 my aunt's birthday; 5 the progress of science; 6 the result of the football match; 7 everybody's darling; 8 the children's toys; 9 my dog's name

3

Horizontal: dentist, chemist, confectioner, greengrocer
Vertikal: butcher, stationer, baker

4

1 stationer's; 2 butcher's; 3 baker's; 4 dentist's; 5 greengrocer's; 6 chemist's; 7 confectioner's

5

Newton's discovery: A
The discovery of Newton: B

6

1 friends'; 2 boss' (*oder:* boss's); 3 bosses'; 4 cats'; 5 Mr and Mrs Jones' (*oder:* Mr and Mrs Jones's); 6 kids'; 7 airlines'; 8 Mr Evans' (*oder:* Mr Evans's); 9 Millers'; 10 parents'

7

1 son; 2 's, father, of his; 3 's, 's, husband, 's, cousin, of mine; 4 brother, 's, of mine, 's, 's, sister-in-law, in-laws, 's

8

1 Scotland's whiskies, The beauty of the hills and lakes; 2 this week's TV guide; 3 a hard day's work; 4 a week's holiday; 5 the quality of our products, This year's sales figures; 6 Britain's youngest Prime Minister, The number of votes

20 Das Substantiv – die Großschreibung

1

1 – f; 2 – d; 3 – h; 4 – a; 5 – g; 6 – i; 7 – b; 8 – c; 9 – e

2

1 Halloween; 2 Thanksgiving Day, Thanksgiving Day; 3 Boxing Day; 4 Independence Day; 5 Valentine's Day; 6 New Year's Day; 7 New Year's Eve; 8 April Fool's Day; 9 Christmas Day

3

1 United Nations Organisation, New York City, organisations, nations; 2 Federal Bureau of Investigation, institution, investigation, state; 3 United States of America, Constitution, states; 4 Wall Street, United States, street, Lower Manhattan, 5 Rocky Mountains, mountain; 6 times, financial, Financial Times, financial; 7 Bank of England, bank, central, bank, United Kingdom; 8 Scottish Whisky Convention, Scottish, whisky, distilleries; 9 British Prime Minister, Downing Street, London, London, Tower, London, tower, Middle Ages, age, centre, city

21 Die Personalpronomen

1
1 I bought it for him. 2 We sold it to them. 3 Could he fetch them for me, please? 4 Get it for her, will you? 5 The shop sells them to you, doesn't it? 6 Could you pass it to him? 7 I gave them to her. 8 Have they received them?

2
1 Take it off! 2 Hang them up on the coat racket over there! 3 Put it off until tomorrow! 4 Don't throw them away! 5 Try them on!

22 Die Possessivpronomen

1
1 their, theirs; 2 their; 3 your, yours, his; 4 theirs, its; 5 our, ours; 6 hers, her; 7 their

2
1 yours; 2 yours, hers; 3 mine, theirs; 4 his, mine

23 Die Reflexivpronomen

1
1 treat yourself; 2 look after ourselves; 3 defend yourself; 4 pay for myself; 5 cut yourself, burn yourself; 6 enjoy yourselves, control yourselves; 7 behave themselves; 8 make a fool of ourselves; 9 Blame yourself; 10 make themselves

24 Die Demonstrativpronomen und -adjektive

1
1 – 2; 2 – 1; 3 – 7; 4 – 5; 5 – 6; 6 – 3; 7 – 4

2
1 this; 2 those; 3 That; 4 Those; 5 This, those; 6 That

25 Die Relativpronomen und Relativsätze

1

1 – 1; 2 – 3; 3 – 2; 4 – 2; 5 – 3; 6 – 1; 7 – 2

2

A – 1; B – 2

3

1 A model, who, which; 2 A catwalk, where; 3 A fashion designer, who; 4 France, where, which; 5 A fashion show, which; 6 A collection, which; 7 Ready-to-wear fashion, which; 8 Fashion week, when

4

1 which shocked the entire neighbourhood. 2 which I find very annoying.
3 which was very rude of him. 4 which was most unfair. 5 which everyone thought was such a pity.

5

1 A UN environmental group warned that eating fish which is caught in polluted rivers and lakes poses a health hazard. 2 Greenpeace, which is an organization for the protection of the environment, called on all governments to issue warnings to consumers. 3 We grieve the death of a child who was killed by a pit bull terrier. 4 60 million land mines, which kill up to 10 people every day, are still scattered around the world. 5 A huge oil spill, which killed thousands of fish and birds, blackened 60 kilometres of coastline in Brazil. 6 Brazil's oil spill, which was the worst (spill) in 25 years, was caused when 4 million litres of oil escaped from a burst pipeline.

6

1 A plane crashed into a residential neighbourhood near Bombay, which led to the killing of 60 people on board and 6 others on the ground. 2 An investigation, which will determine the cause of the accident, is still underway. 3 The crash has raised questions about the safety procedures for India's planes, which sometimes are called coffins in the air because of their bad record. 4 In 1986 Swedish technicians recorded levels of radiation, which was the beginning of the worst crisis in the history of nuclear power plants. 5 Fourteen years after the worst radiation accident in history, which had taken place at the Chernobyl power station, the remaining working reactor will be closed.

26 Die unbestimmten Pronomen (*some, any, much, many,* usw.)

1
1 How many people does your company employ? 2 How much money do your secretaries earn per month? 3 How many hours per day do your employees work? 4 How much time do your workers have for their lunch breaks? 5 How many holidays per year are they entitled to? 6 How much flexibility do you allow your workers?

2
1 few; 2 little; 3 few; 4 few; 5 much; 6 a lot of; 7 few

3
1 little, much; 2 few; 3 little; 4 few, many; 5 little, much; 6 few; 7 little, much

4
1 a lot of, many; 2 a lot of, much; 3 a lot of, much; 4 much, many, a lot; 5 a lot of, many; 6 a lot, many, much; 7 much, much, much

5
1 Yesterday's meeting was a disaster. There weren't any questions we wanted them to answer. 2 They didn't have any time left. They didn't explain anything in detail. (*oder:* They had no time left to explain anything in detail.) 3 The managing director didn't tell us any interesting facts about the project. 4 I hadn't read any of their reports. 5 I didn't ask for any additional information about their company. 6 Unfortunately, they had some problems with their new computers. 7 That's why they couldn't print any information about their sales figures and the staff.

6
1 some; 2 some; 3 any; 4 some; 5 any; 6 some; 7 some; 8 some; 9 some; 10 any; 11 some; 12 some; 13 some; 14 some; 15 any; 16 any; 17 some

27 Die Fragewörter

1
1 – d; 2 – e; 3 – b; 4 – f; 5 – g; 6 – c; 7 – a

2
1 Who; 2 What; 3 Who; 4 Where; 5 What; 6 What

3

1 How; 2 How; 3 What; 4 When; 5 Whose; 6 How

4

1 What is your name? First name and surname, please. 2 When were you born? (*oder:* What is your date of birth?). 3 Where were you born? (*oder:* What is your place of birth?) 4 What is your marital status? 5 What nationality are you? 6 What is your address and phone number? (*oder:* Where do you live? What is your phone number?) 7 Do you have children? 8 What do you do? (*oder:* What's your occupation?)

5

1 – b; 2 – d; 3 – a; 4 – c

6

1 What, It is 5 past 10. 2 When, The plane leaves at 10 am. 3 How long, It takes you approximately three quarters of an hour (*oder:* 45 minutes). 4 When, The next train to Liverpool is at 8 o'clock. 5 What, Today is Monday. (*oder:* It's Monday.) 6 What, It's 5th June, 2000. (*oder:* the fifth of June 2000; June the 5th 2000). 7 When, The concert (*oder:* It) starts at 8 pm.

7

1 What is your name, please? 2 How do you spell Meier? (*oder:* Could you spell your name, please?) 3 How old are you? (*oder:* What is your age?) 4 What nationality are you? 5 When will you arrive? (*oder:* What will be the date of arrival?) 6 What will be the exact time of arrival? (*oder:* When exactly will you arrive?) 7 How long will you stay? (*oder:* How long are you going to stay? How long do you plan to stay?) 8 When will you leave? (*oder:* What will be the date of departure?) 9 Which type of accommodation do you require?

8

1 How many rooms does your hotel have? (*oder:* do you have?); 2 How many rooms with private bathrooms do you have? (*oder:* How many rooms have a private bathroom? Do you have any rooms with private bathrooms? Do all the rooms have a private bathroom?) 3 Do all the rooms have TV? 4 How long is the walk to the beach? 5 When do you serve breakfast? (*oder:* When is breakfast?) 6 How much does a single room cost? (*oder:* How much is a single room?) 7 How much does a single room with bathroom cost? (*oder:* How much is a single room with bathroom?) 8 Are dogs welcome?

28 Das Adjektiv und das Adverb

1
1 terribly; 2 wonderful; 3 absolutely; 4 simply; 5 really; 6 unfortunately; 7 late; 8 immediately

2
1 stressful; 2 literally; 3 thick; 4 gorgeous; 5 fantastic; 6 actually; 7 awful; 8 already; 9 sadly; 10 trendy; 11 volume-enhancing; 12 extremely; 13 expensive; 14 quick; 15 desperate; 16 soon

3
Dear Jane, Hair normally grows 1 cm per month. In summer it possibly grows a little faster. You can't accelerate this natural process. Unfortunately you have to be very patient. Wear a beautiful scarf to cover up your hairdo. Or why don't you try a fashionable hat? Try not to be so hysterical and nervous. Go and see a good psychiatrist. Yours Nelly

4
1 successfully; 2 extraordinarily; 3 very well; 4 enthusiastically; 5 frenetically

5
1 just; 2 nearly; 3 straight; 4 near; 5 far; 6 lately; 7 late; 8 most; 9 mostly; 10 hardly; 11 hard; 12 shortly; 13 short

6
1 felt sick; 2 sound wonderful; 3 smell gorgeous; 4 looks – spectacular; 5 tastes awful

7
1 hardly; 2 hardly; 3 hard; 4 justly; 5 just; 6 justly; 7 just; 8 near; 9 nearly; 10 nearly; 11 lately; 12 late

8
1 taller; 2 brighter; 3 higher; 4 darker

9

	Jane	Jill	Julia
income	\$200m	\$30m	\$130m
age	87 years	36	53
weight	80 kilos	79	98
size	5 ft 4	5 ft 10	6 ft 2
frame of mind	happy	quite happy	not very happy

10

1 richest; 2 heaviest; 3 Jane; 4 Julia; 5 Julia, Jane; 6 Jill, Jane; 7 Jill, Julia, Jane; 8 Julia, Jill, Jane; 9 Jill, Julia, Jane

11

1 safer than; 2 quieter than; 3 more expensive than; 4 as entertaining as; 5 as informative as

12

popular; boring; exciting; gentle; funny; pretty; sophisticated; good

13

1 most popular; 2 most boring; 3 most exciting; 4 gentlest; 5 funniest (funny); 6 prettiest (pretty); 7 best (good); 8 most sophisticated

14

1 The more I got to know him, the more I appreciated his good manners.
2 The thicker the coat, the warmer it'll keep you in winter.
3 The more you have, the more you want.
4 The older the wine, the bigger the taste.
5 The longer she had to wait, the more nervous she became.
6 The more you buy, the heavier the shopping bag.
7 The more you try, the more likely you are to succeed.

15

1 – f, 2 – b, 3 – g, 4 – c, 5 – d, 6 – e, 7 – a, 8 – h

16

1 Not only did he have me waiting for half an hour, he didn't even bother apologizing to me when he finally arrived. 2 Not only was he very rude to the waiter, he upset all the other guests by being so noisy and telling them to shut up. 3 Not only was the main topic of conversation, of course, himself, he also accused me of not being able to listen to other people's problems. 4 Not only

was he eating noisily, he also was talking with his mouth full. 5 Not only did he forget his credit card, he also had no cash with him. 6 Not only did I have to pay for the meal, he also asked me if I could lend him some money. 7 Not only was he drunk, he asked me if I could get him a taxi and pay for it. 8 Not only was this the most embarrassing date I've ever had, it was also one of the costliest.

29 Die Präpositionen

1

1 on; 2 on; 3 off; 4 in; 5 in; 6 on; 7 in; 8 to

2

1 in; 2 in; 3 in; 4 on; 5 in; 6 at; 7 in; 8 in; 9 at; 10 on; 11 in; 12 On; 13 at; 14 at; 15 at; 16 At; 17 in; 18 in; 19 in

3

1 at, in; 2 on (*oder:* in), at; 3 at; 4 at, in; 5 at (*oder:* as of)

4

1 in; 2 in; 3 in; 4 on; 5 in; 6 at; 7 from, to (*oder:* till); 8 at; 9 in; 10 at, at; 11 in, in; 12 on, at, in

5

1 Go down this road. Go straight down this road. Keep straight on. 2 Turn right. 3 When you get to the church, turn left. 4 Turn right at the crossing. 5 Take the second turning to the left. 6 You'll see the bank on your left.

30 Die Zahlen

1

1 The First Wives Club, First; 2 The Second Man; 3 Third, The Third Man; 4 Fourth; 5 The Fifth Element; 6 Sixth; 7 The Seventh Cross; 8 Bluebeard's Eighth Wife; 9 Ninth; 10 Thirteenth

2

1 add up to; 2 multiplied by; 3 is divisable by; 4 divided by; equals; 5 minus; 6 multiplied by; 7 minus; 8 plus

3

What (*oder:* How) about February, 14 (“fourteen”) (*oder:* 14th (“fourteenth”) February, “the fourteenth of February”) at one p.m. (*oder:* one o’clock in the afternoon)?
That’s not possible, sorry.
My plane doesn’t land until noon (*oder* 12 (“twelve”) o’clock), and driving from the airport to the city takes me approximately 1 (“one”) hour and 40 (“fourty”) minutes.
But we could meet in a café late in the afternoon.
I’m sorry, but I have a meeting at quarter past 5 (“five”) in the afternoon.
Can’t you postpone it?
Unfortunately, no (*oder:* not).
It’s a meeting with one of our most important customers.
He buys goods to the value of 1.57 (“one point five seven”) billion dollars.
This accounts for (*oder:* corresponds to) two thirds of our total annual turnover (*oder:* sales).
We could meet for a tennis match on May 1 (“one”) (*oder:* 1st (“first”) May, “May the first”, the first of May).
That’s not possible.
It’s my boss’s (*oder:* boss’) birthday.
He’ll be 80 (“eighty”).
At the same time we’re celebrating the thirtieth anniversary of the company.
Perhaps I’ll have (*oder:* I might have) time in a fortnight.
How about dinner? On Wednesday, February 3 (“three”) (*oder:* 3rd February, “the third of February”)?
That’s fine with me (*oder:* suits me fine).
There is a new restaurant in 15 (“fifteen”), Neal Street.
On foot it’s 10 (“ten”) minutes away from here.
Just walk to the crossing and take the 4th (“fourth”) street on your left.
It is an old house built in 1899.
The café is on the 3rd (“third”) floor. It’s called TIME OUT.

4

1 number one; 2 seventh heaven; 3 two and two; 4 one in a million; 5 two-faced; 6 sixth sense; 7 sixes and sevens; 8 first; 9 six of one and half a dozen of the other; 10 seven-year-itch; 11 first come, first served

5

A 1 – c, 2 – a, 3 – b; B 1 – b, 2 – c, 3 – a; C 1 – b, 2 – c, 3 – a; D 1 – b, 2 – c, 3 – a; E 1 – c, 2 – a, 3 – b

Grammatische Fachausdrücke

Adjektiv, Eigenschaftswort; *adjective:* ***hot*** *water,* heißes Wasser
Adverb, Umstandswort; *adverb: very good,* sehr gut
Artikel, Geschlechtswort; *article:* ***a*** *friend,* ein Freund; ***the*** *car,* das Auto
Futur, Zukunft, *future: he* ***will go,*** er wird gehen; *he* ***will have gone,*** er wird gegangen sein
Future, Futur I: *he* ***will go,*** er wird gehen
Future Perfect, Futur II: ***he will have asked,*** er wird gefragt haben
Genitiv, 2. Fall, Wesfall, *genitive:* ***the woman's bag,*** die Tasche der Frau
Gerundium, gebeugte Grundform des Zeitwortes, *gerund:* ***Swimming*** *is healthy. (Das)* Schwimmen ist gesund.
if*-Satz**, Bedingungssatz, *if-clause:* ***If I were a rich man I'd buy you a castle. Wenn ich reich wäre, würde ich dir ein Schloss kaufen.
Imperativ, Befehlsform, *imperative:* ***Open the window!*** Öffne das Fenster!
indirekte Rede, wiedergegebene Rede, *reported speech:* ***She said that she saw the plane.*** Sie sagte, sie sehe das Flugzeug.
Infinitiv, Grundform, *infinitive:* ***to sing,*** singen
ing-form, *progressive form,* Verlaufsform: *I* ***was drinking,*** ich trank (gerade)
Konjunktiv, Möglichkeitsform, *subjunctive: I wish it* **were** *over*. Ich wünschte, es wäre vorbei.
Passiv, Leideform, *passive voice:* ***we were punished,*** wir wurden bestraft
Past Perfect, Plusquamperfekt: *I* ***had eaten,*** ich hatte gegessen
Past Tense, Vergangenheit: *she* ***saw,*** sie sah
Personalpronomen, persönliches Fürwort, *personal pronoun:* ***he,*** er
Phrasal Verb, *I* ***look forward to*** *your letter.* Ich freue mich auf Ihren Brief.
Plural, Mehrzahl, *plural:* ***men,*** Männer
Possessivpronomen, besitzanzeigendes Fürwort, *possessive adjective:* ***my, your***; *possessive pronoun:* ***mine, yours***
Präposition, Verhältniswort, *preposition:* ***on*** *the table,* auf dem Tisch
Präsens, Gegenwart, *present tense: He* ***sings*** *a song.* Er singt ein Lied.
Present Participle, Partizip I: *I can see him* ***crossing*** *the road*. Ich kann sehen, wie er die Straße überquert.
Present Perfect, Perfekt, Vollendung in der Gegenwart: *I* ***have bought*** *a car.* Ich habe ein Auto gekauft.
Reflexivpronomen, rückbezügliches Fürwort, *reflexive pronoun: I made it* ***myself.*** Ich habe es selbst gemacht.
Substantiv, Hauptwort, *noun:* ***cow,*** Kuh
Superlativ, höchste Steigerungsstufe, *superlative degree: the* **best** *writer,* der beste Schriftsteller

Synonym, *synonym*: ***Small** and **little** are synonyms.* 'Small' und 'little' sind Synonyme.

unvollständiges Hilfsverben, *defective auxiliaries: You **may** enter now.* Sie dürfen jetzt hineingehen.

Verb, Zeitwort, *verb: **go**,* gehen

Verlaufsform, *ing-form, progressive form: I was **drinking**,* ich trank (gerade)